Title: **Contemporary Methods of Digitization**

Subtitle: **Digitization process, archival methods and documentation of films, photographs and various other conventional and digital sources.**

Writer: Panagiotis M. Zigouris
Editor: Panagiotis M. Zigouris

ISBN: 978-618-84900-1-7
EDITOR: Panagiotis M. Zigouris
Translation from Greek: Panagiotis Zigouris
Original Title: Διαδικασία ψηφιοποίησης, μέθοδοι αρχειοθέτησης και τεκμηρίωσης, διαφόρων συμβατικών και ψηφιακών πηγών.

Information:
www.texnikos-ipologiston.gr
info@texnikos-ipologiston.gr
+30 6975964828

https://www.facebook.com/texnikosipologiston/

https://www.instagram.com/texnikosipologiston/

https://twitter.com/TexnikosPCtech

1st edition in English language: April 2020

2

To my parents and my family

INSTEAD OF A PROLOGUE

A book missing from the internet.

Nowadays where technology is advancing at a fast pace, it is a fact that many technologies are becoming obsolete immediately and many data, analogue and digital based on these, are becoming inaccessible and will be lost permanently.

Every day a large number of photos either in the form of print or digital from legacy devices, files, videos etc. are deleted or destroyed without any substantive method of recovering them. This phenomenon occurs not only privately but also in the public sector, in companies, archives, libraries, and in almost any form where archival material exists.

Digitizing, archiving and documenting.

This book describes a fully documented and thorough method of digitizing, archiving, and documenting material from various digital and analog sources. In order to save this material from deleting, destroying or storing it in inaccessible sources and media, and to create digital libraries with a structured, and most likely long-term, future use.

What can you expect.

You will not find historical data on file storage formats or other issues, as well as analysis of handling old devices and methods as this is not its purpose. Only information necessary to substantiate the procedures is provided.

There are many methods of digitization available for us, but there are no substantial and detailed ones adapted to our needs. The book is about to fill that gap.

The book was completed in 2019 after three years of research, (with some corrections and additions in 2020) and published in April, 2020.

Panagiotis Zigouris

info@texnikos-ipologiston.gr

Contents

NOTE

Websites and pages are constantly changing either by moving, alternation or content update, by migrating or by becoming dead links after a long time. I had personally made a digital copy of all websites I am referring to this book using the Wayback Machine. www.webarchive.org.

All you have to do is copy and page the link to their page to see the archived version.

For webpages depicting information or products that archiving was not possible (e-shops like Amazon or eBay) or other type of dynamic pages I provide search keyword to Google it / Bing it.

I believe that in such manner the book becomes future proof to some point.

Wayback Machine can be used also for your personal needs e.g., to store your own webpages in case your site eventually shuts down or for webpages that you particularly want to store for indefinite time for archival purposes or for providing future references to those.

CHAPTER ONE

THE PROJECT WITH DATA AND NUMBERS

An introduction:

Photos, negatives, videotapes, vinyl records, etc. must be digitized, now or even yesterday. Humidity and many other factors, environmental and non-environmental, work against them.

Tomorrow, in a month, in a year, etc. they may no longer have the same quality or be completely lost.

1. EQUIPMENT

Without substantially expensive equipment I was able to produce professional-grade material. This was, after all, a bet that this kind of work can be done in the home environment without having to resort to expensive solutions such as photo and negative scanning services and above all to create a fully structured and functional digital archive with own means. In detail the equipment used, below.

2. SCANNER

With an average price in 2019 of 155 to 180 euros, the Epson Perfection V370 Photo is an option for daily use, with the capability of scanning negatives. Epson's perfection series consists of models ranging from simple use to V550, V700, V750, V800 and the V850 flagship model, which are purely for professional use.

The V370 is the first of a series that can be used for demanding tasks such as this project and is also a cost-effective solution, without lag and potentially reliable since, as I mentioned later in the statistics, it carried out about 18000 scans and it continues to work smoothly.

Tech Specs:

Epson® Perfection® V370 Photo

Technology

Scanner type
Flatbed scanner
Scanning Resolution
4.800 DPI (Horizontal x Vertical)
Optical Resolution
Main 4.800 DPI x Sub 9.600 DPI
Optical Density
3,2 Dmax
Paper Formats
A4
Colour Depth
Input: 48 Bits Colour , Output: 48 Bits Colour
Application
High Resolution

Scanner

Optical Sensor
Matrix CCD
Light Source
LED ReadyScan Technology
Scanning Method
Fixed document and moving carriage
Output Resolution
50~6400 (1 dpi step), 9600, (12800 DPI with digital enhancing)

Paper and Media handling

Document size - Flatbed A4

Supported film - TPU
35mm strip film: 6 frames, 35mm mounted film: 4 frames

Scanning Features

Features
RGB colour dropout, Automatic area segmentation, RGB colour enhance, Text enhancement, Unsharp Mask (USM)
Output formats
BMP, JPEG, TIFF, multi-TIFF, PDF, searchable PDF

Connectivity

Connectivity
USB 2.0 Type B

Operating System

Compatible Operating Systems
Mac OS 10.5.8 or later, Windows 10, Windows 7, Windows 7 x64, Windows Vista, Windows Vista x64, Windows XP, Windows XP x64

Information from EPSON's official page

https://www.epson.eu/en_EU/products/scanners/consumer/perfection-v370-photo/p/12034

3. COMPUTER

Intel i5 4th generation with 8GB of memory, Windows 7, SSD, and 4TB conventional (mechanical) disk, NVidia GeForce GTX 1060Ti graphics card and 4K (DELL S2817Q) monitor

The process could be done with both Windows 10, Windows 11 and Windows XP, as long as the scanner is compatible. Windows XP does not support NVidia 1060.

In newer generations of processors there is no driver support for Windows XP and very difficult to obtain support also for Windows 7.

4. PROJECT MATERIAL

In the project I had to work with:

- 75, 26mm (126) films shot from 1969 to 2003 with the same camera (Instamatic 133X)

http://camera-wiki.org/wiki/Kodak_Instamatic_133_Camera

- 4, 35mm (135) films shot with the Canon Prima Super 105u from 2003 to 2006

https://global.canon/en/c-museum/product/film239.html

(Camera specification, shutter speed, etc. can be found in the links above. I don't think it's a question of comparing capabilities at the moment when we have two cameras designed for non-professional use, with a technological distance of almost 35 years)

- Color and black and white photographs, with different surfaces (matte, glossy, etc.) ranging from 1903 to 2006.
- Documents (almost all of A4 size with slight fluctuations) and aged from 1852 to 2019.

5. BUILD FOR THE FUTURE

To the question what does "Build for the future" mean in a web search we will find many results.

But the classic answer is: We are rebuilding the present to provide better infrastructure for future generations. This can also be interpreted as "We learn from our mistakes not to repeat them in the future". The definition can go a long way but in general the first one is the accepted interpretation.

My purpose is not to analyze the philosophical implications of the subject but to apply it to the specific subject of my research. So, in this case the wording is: Creating files and how to archive and document them, which will be accessible, understandable and usable by future generations.

6. SIZE AND FILE RESOLUTION

Scanning a photo at 300 dpi, as recommended by photographers, (or at most 400) the file created provides enough quality to make a duplicate copy, and as mentioned below, already printed photos are of no greater quality than that.

Scanning a 10x15 photo at 300 dpi creates a 1802x1177 file that on a 1920x1080 Full HD resolution screen almost fills the screen.

But it won't continue to fill up when the resolution goes up to 4K, 8K or larger screen resolutions that will appear in the future.

To give an example, an average photo from the era of computers running Windows 98 or XP (30 years for Windows 98 or nearly 20 years for XP) has a resolution of 300x200 pixels. On a high resolution 800x600 screen, the photo captured 1/3 of the screen.

However, at a resolution of 1920x1080 the photo does not take more than 1/6 and when zoom in, we see only magnified pixels. (the "Pixelation" phenomenon)

If we try to view the same photo on a 4K screen, it will not be larger than a stamp. So scanning at 300 dpi is good enough for today, but totally inadequate for tomorrow, when our goal is to create a digital file.

Scanning on the other hand at 1200 dpi for a 10x15 photo (which is also the resolution we prefer for photos) produces a 7209x4710 file size almost equal to 8K resolution.

So, it is automatically considered suitable for digital archive as it covers the largest applied screen resolution in the market so far. (Commercially available, there are larger ones).

Although the resolutions will continue to go up, the file's viability is assured in the future, since such a size, 48bit color depth and in TIFF format, as we will see below, is usable, and largely functional in many respects, at great depth of time.

In fact, mobile phones with a resolution of over 48MP (megapixels) and digital cameras with an even greater market share have now been released. There have been many who comment that "unless you plan to print your photos on enlarged sizes or posters, these resolutions are useless"

As I have already described above this is huge nonsense. We should always use mobile phones or and cameras with the highest resolution (which we can at least buy) since large resolutions are essentially a legacy for the future.

This is also the application of the "Build for the Future" concept to the digitization and archiving of photographs we are negotiating.

High-definition			
Name	H (px)	V (px)	H:V	H × V (Mpx)
nHD	640	360	16:9	0.230
qHD	960	540	16:9	0.518
HD	1280	720	16:9	0.922
HD+	1600	900	16:9	1.440
FHD	1920	1080	16:9	2.074
(W)QHD	2560	1440	16:9	3.686
QHD+	3200	1800	16:9	5.760
4K UHD	3840	2160	16:9	8.294
5K	5120	2880	16:9	14.746
8K UHD	7680	4320	16:9	33.178

Digital resolutions with absolute number of pixels

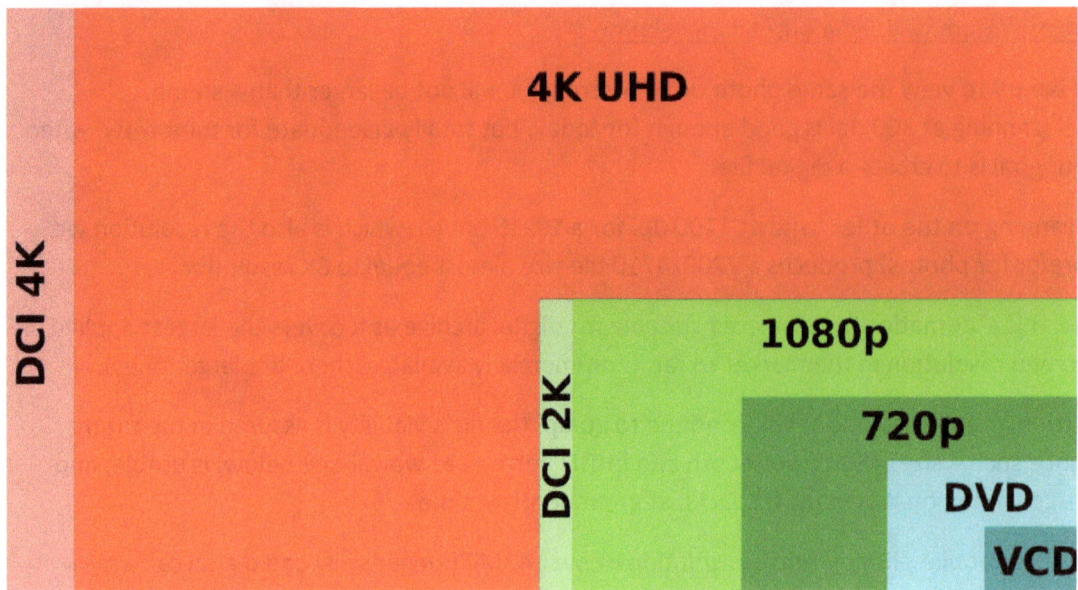

Picture 1: Size of the most common digital tile screen resolutions

By TRauMa - Own work, CC0,
https://commons.wikimedia.org/w/index.php?curid=19203438

7. JPG AND TIFF

A brief reference to JPG and TIFF

JPG is the format most images on the web and social media belong to. Released in 1992, it quickly became popular due to its ability to create small files and was first released in 1992. JPG is lossless, meaning it removes "useless" data from the file, compressing its size without compromising quality. of the image, at least not visually and to a small degree of compression.

As we increase the compression rate, information is lost and after one certain point the image quality deteriorates.

There is no uncompressed JPG file, since even if we set the compression to 0, data will still be lost.

The JPG also has a maximum color depth of 24bit * 3 channels of R + B + G x 8-bit color for each color = 24bit

Data is also lost during file editing, even if we use applications that perform lossless editing

These are all about JPG that concern us. For the full story of the JPG and its features you can refer to the link below.

https://en.wikipedia.org/wiki/JPEG

TIFF is older and was created in 1986. It is mainly aimed at professionals (photographers, graphic designers, etc.) and unlike JPG, TIFF files have no compression and therefore no loss of information.

The files can also be edited continuously without losing their quality.

It has great features and has a huge scope of applications.

TIFF also has a maximum color depth of 48bit * 3 color channels R + B + G x 16 bit to each color = 48bit

The creation of a lossless quality file and color depth are what we require most.

The only downside is creating huge files since no compression is applied.

For a full list of its features in the link below.

https://en.wikipedia.org/wiki/TIFF

So undoubtedly is recommended the use of TIFF with a 48bit color depth.

8. RESOLUTION (COLOR DEPTH) 24 and 48bit

Without many technical details, the definition of Color Depth follows

The color of an image is based on the 3 color channels, Red, Green, Blue (Red Green Blue - RGB)

Each color channel contains bits (color information)

The JPG also has a maximum color depth of 24bit * 3 channels of R + B + G x 8-bit color to each color = 24bit

TIFF also has a maximum color depth of 48bit * 3 channels of color R + B + G x 16 bit to each color = 48bit

Simply put, what's the difference between a 24-bit and a 48-bit scan?

Scanning at 24 bits we get less color information (bits) per channel and therefore less color quality of our digital images.

For the color depth in detail in the link below

https://en.wikipedia.org/wiki/Color_depth

Even simpler:

https://howtoscan.ca/scanning-tips/difference-between-24-bit-vs-48-bit-scans.php

Although scanning the material at 48bit as I have already mentioned in Build for the Future is one-way, its visualization is not a simple affair, at least not for most.

It is practically impossible to see a difference between 24bit and 48bit color since the vast majority of computer and TV screens cannot display 48bit color which is still used almost purely for business purposes.

Most modern computers have a color resolution of between 24 and 32 bits, provided the monitor has also this capability.

Even with a GeForce GTX 1060Ti graphics card and a 4K display (DELL S2817Q) the maximum color depth is 30bit (bpp - bit per pixel) / 10bpc (10 bit per channel), i.e., true 30bit color.

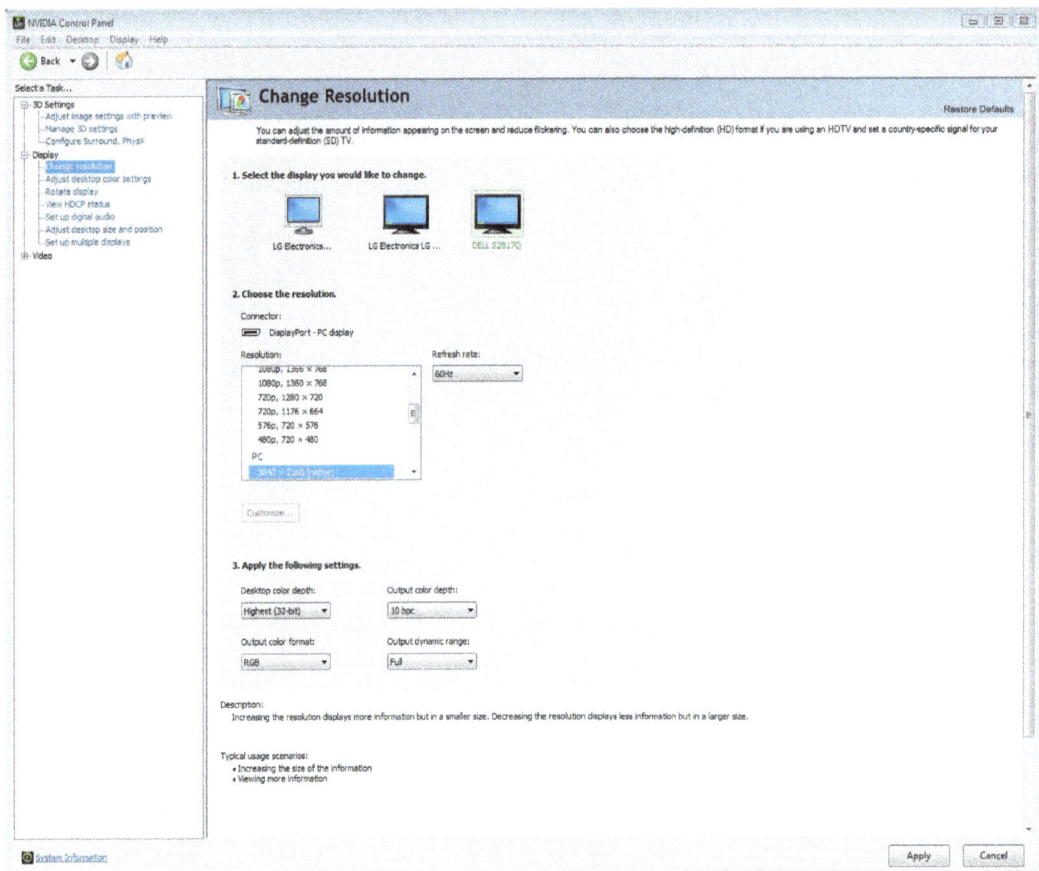

Picture 2: NVidia Control Panel where among others with can set the color depth to 10bpc

However, the difference from a simple display to the colors is really impressive.

Of course, applications that can display 10bpc colors are minimal. The test was done with Photoshop (trial) and ACDSee.

More than 32bit / 10 bpc color depth requires specialized graphics cards such as AMD Radeon Pro and Nvidia Quadro, Display Port connectivity and a corresponding 12, 14 or 16 bpc capable screen display for professional use as well.

Bits / Pixel (bpp)	Bits / Red Channel (bpc)	Bits / Green Channel (bpc)	Bits / Blue Channel (bpc)	Number of available colors	Display name
1				2	Monochrome
8	3	3	2	256	VGA
12	4	4	4	4096	Super VGA
16	5	5	6	65536	XGA, High Color
24	8	8	8	16777216	SVGA, True Color
30	10	10	10	1 billion	Deep Color
36	12	12	12	68 billion	Deep Color
48	16	16	16	281 trillion	Deep Color

14

Indicative table with the number of colors per channel and the total number of colors available

Accordingly, color differences and photo and scanning quality cannot be printed in the written version of this book since the usual book printing quality does not exceed 400dpi.

This feature is only available in the electronic version, since of course the corresponding pdf file has been created in high resolution and if as I mentioned above, the computer is capable of 4K imaging in 30bit color or more and several other parameters are met.

Note: The human eye too can only distinguish about 10 million different colors. So, by creating a photo with a color depth greater than 24bit you will not see more colors.

The difference is with the color palette that since it has greater color depth, it can display more accurate and vibrant colors in the photo. Also, photos with a color depth of over 24bit can be processed in a second time, giving much better results.

9. SIZE, STATISTICS, TIMES AND TOTAL SIZE ON DISK

Here are some subtotal and total values of sizes, statistics, times, and disk space required to scan

- **76 Negative films 126**

63 X 24 poses 1512 (excluding 86 blank frames, 1426)

13 x 12 Poses 156 (excluding 19 blank frames, 137)

1563 frames total

x 2 scans (with and without color restoration, in tiff, 3126)

x 2 scan (with and without color restoration, in jpg, 3126)

Total 6252 scanned frames

6252 scans x 1'37 " minutes for each at 4800dpi, 8565 min, 142.75 hours
x about 3 minutes for storage, naming, archiving and documentation, 18756 minutes, 312.6 hours

Subtotal for scanning 126 films: 455.35 hours or 19 days

Disk Space: 440.6 GB

- **4 Negative films 135**

x 36 poses, 144 (excluding 9 blank frames, 135)

x 2 scans (with and without color restoration, in tiff, 270)

x 2 scan (with and without color restoration, in jpg, 270)

540 frames total

540 min x 1'59 "min for each scan at 4800dpi, 858.6 min, 35.77 h
x about 3 minutes for storage, naming, archiving and documentation, 1620 minutes, 27 hours

Subtotal for scanning 135 films: 62.77 hours or 2.6 days

Disk Space: 85 GB

Grand total for scanning all negatives: 518.1 hours, 21.6 days

Disk Space: 525.6 GB

- **229 black and white photos of various sizes (from 19x28 cm to 3x3 cm)**

Approximate horizontal scan time at 1200dpi for each photo 55 seconds,

x 2 scans (with and without color restoration, in tiff, 458)

x 2 scan (with and without color restoration, in jpg, 458)

Total 916 photos x 55" per scan at 1200 dpi, 503.8 minutes 8.39 hours

x about 3 minutes for storage, naming, archiving and documentation, 2748 minutes, 45.8 hours, 1.90 days

Partial set for black and white photos: 3251.8 minutes, 54.1 hours, 2.25 days

Disk Space: 74.3 GB

- **741 color photos of 126 10x10cm films**

x 2 scans (with and without color restoration, in tiff, 1482)
x 2 scan (with and without color restoration, in jpg, 1482)

Total 2964 x 46 "photos per scan at 1200 dpi, 1363.44 minutes, 22.72 hours

x about 3 minutes for storage, naming, archiving and documentation 8892 minutes, 148.2 hours 2.47 days

Subtotal for 10x10cm color photos: 10255 minutes, 170 hours, 7.12 days

Disk Space: 137 GB

- **116 color photographs of 135 films 10x15cm in size**

x 2 scans (with and without color restoration, in tiff, 232)
x 2 scan (with and without color restoration, in jpg, 232)

Total 464 x 46 "photos per scan at 1200 dpi, 213.44 minutes, 3.55 hours

x about 3 minutes for storage, naming, archiving and documentation 1392 minutes, 23.2 hours

Subtotal for 10x15 color photos: 1605.44 minutes, 26.75 hours, 1.11 days

Disk space: 32.5 GB

Grand total for scanning all photos: 15111 minutes, 250.85 hours, 10.48 days

• **1271 pages of A4 size at 600dpi X 1 scan at 24bit jpg, 444.85 minutes 7.41 hours**

x about 3 minutes for storage, naming, archiving and documentation 3813 minutes, 63 hours, 2.62 days

Subtotal for A4 pages: 4257.85 minutes 70.96 hours, 2.95 days

Disk Space: 18.61 GB

Grand Total for all scans: 12407, if we also include test and non-successful scan attempts, the number is around 18,000.

* The 3 minutes time per photo or page includes storage, archiving and documentation, storing the file on the disk, crop or rotating it, storing it to another location (another folder or hard drive) its proper name and description, (what is depicted, who appears) and its documentation (time frame, location, historical background, etc.)

GRAND TOTAL OF TIME REQUIRED FOR SCANNING, ARCHIVING AND DOCUMENTATION					
TYPE	MINUTES	HOURS	DAYS		SPACE ON DISK (IN GB)
76 NEGATIVES 126	27321	455,4	19		440,6
4 NEGATIVES 135	1620	62,77	2,6		85
	28941	**518,1**	**21,6**		**525,6**
229 BLACK AND WHITE PHOTOS	**3251**	**54,1**	**2,25**		**74,3**
741 COLOR PHOTOS 10x10	10255	170	7,12		137
116 COLOR PHOTOS 10x15	1605	26,75	1,11		32,5
	11860	**250,9**	**10,48**		**243,8**
1271 PAGES A4 SIZE A4	**4257**	**79,96**	**2,95**		**18,61**
GRAND TOTAL	**48309**	**903**	**37,28**		**862,3**

CHAPTER TWO

PHOTO SCAN

10. FILM 135 SCANNING - PROCEDURE, METHODS AND RESULTS

As I've already mentioned the scanner has native capability of scanning only 135 negative films, so things are easy here as not all the adjustments and settings I applied to the 126 films are required.

Here are the scan results in all available methods

1. Full Auto Mode.

The Full Auto Scan mode can only work for 135 films (even then you must switch to Professional (manual mode) to select filters. In photo scan also cannot focus accurately on the photo edges and many times crops a portion of the photo, therefore is not recommended.

2.Professional (manual) Mode.

We place the negative in the film holder that comes with the scanner and the result we have on our screen is the following. Many additional options and controls are provided.

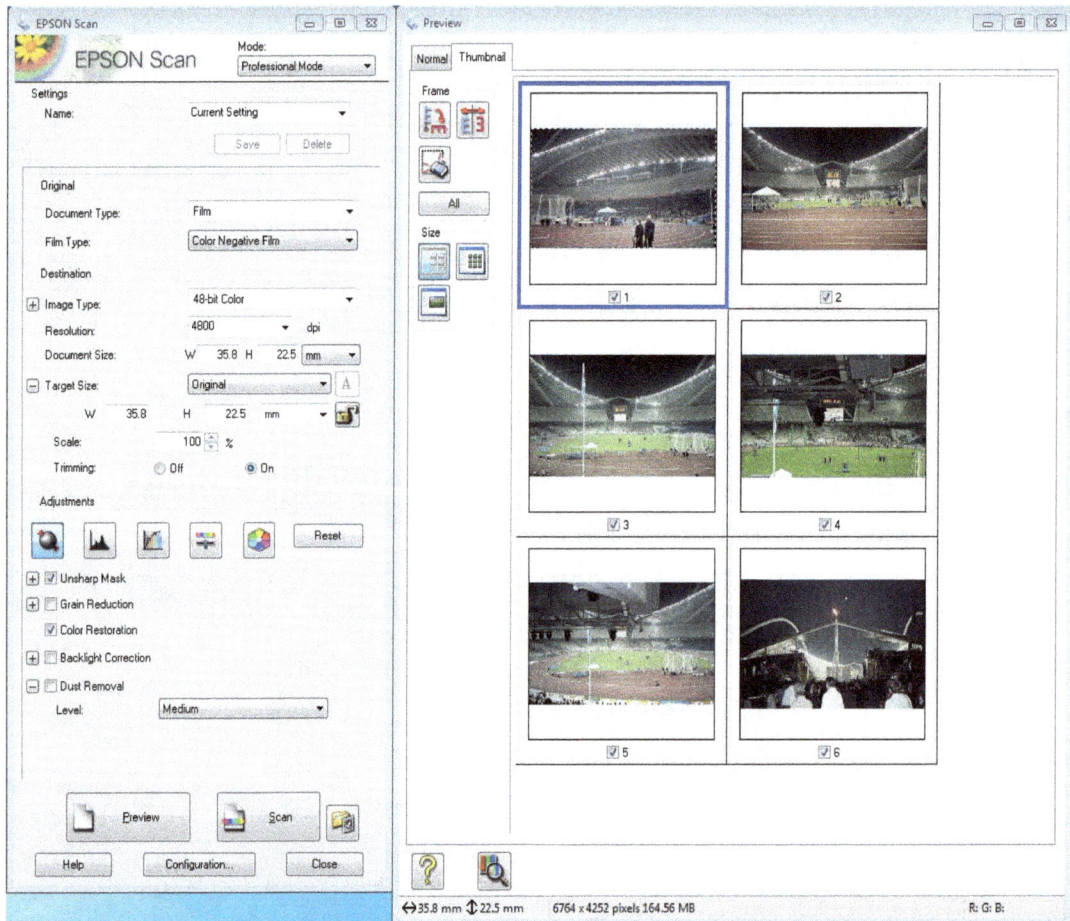

Picture 3: The Professional (manual) mode at 4800 dpi resolution gives us a picture of about 6768 x 4288 pixels almost twice the 4k resolution (4096 × 2160) and a bit smaller

than the 8K UHD resolution (7680 × 4320) at 9600 dpi; the image dimension is projected at about 13151x8576

From this screen we select the frame we want and the program starts scanning.

The enhancements I chose were: Unsharp Mask and Color Restoration.

Picture 4. 135 film negatives placed on the film holder

Picture 5. The image produced by the automatic scan procedure with selected enhancements

Then I removed the image enhancements to see the differences in the result as in the 126 films.

Picture 6. Image with Color Restoration without Unsharp Mask

Picture 7. Image without Color Restoration and Unsharp Mask. There is a clear difference between a scan from a negative with a Color Restoration and a printed photo. As in the case of the 126 film though, we apply also double scans, with Color Restoration and without, for archiving and documentation purposes, always at 4800 dpi and TIFF 48bit color.

Then I scanned again manually (Professional Mode) but with selecting "Normal" instead of the "Thumbnail" preview. Manual scanning through "Normal" preview was one-way for the 126 films.

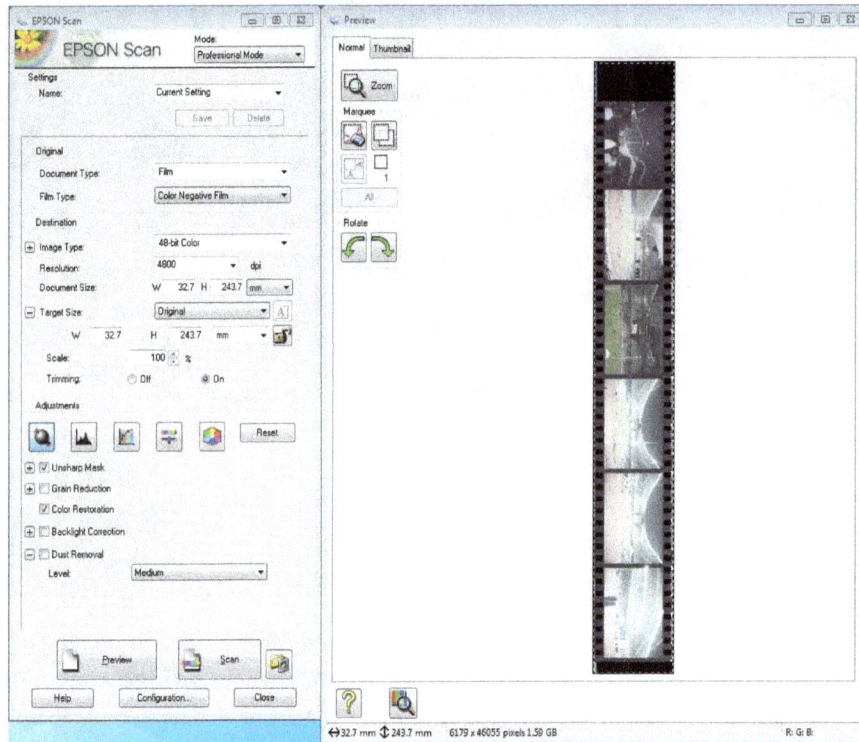

Picture 8. Without having selected a particular frame, the program cannot focus and refine the coloring through the enhancement filters are selected.

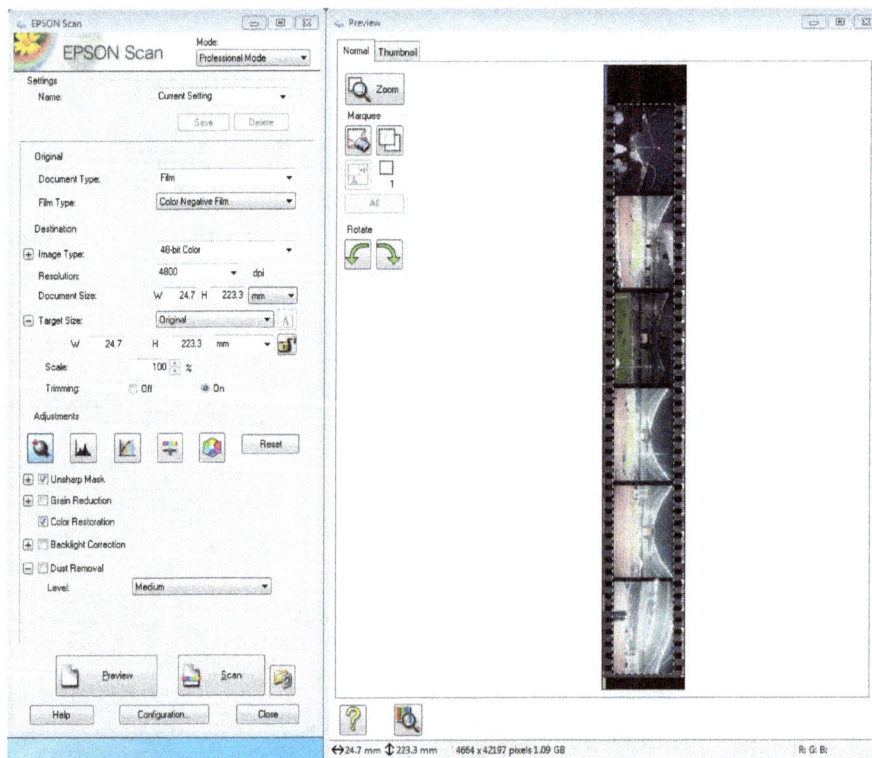

Picture 9. By selecting all the positive negatives without their edges, we get an improvement in the colors created by the filters but without again rendering the color correctly.

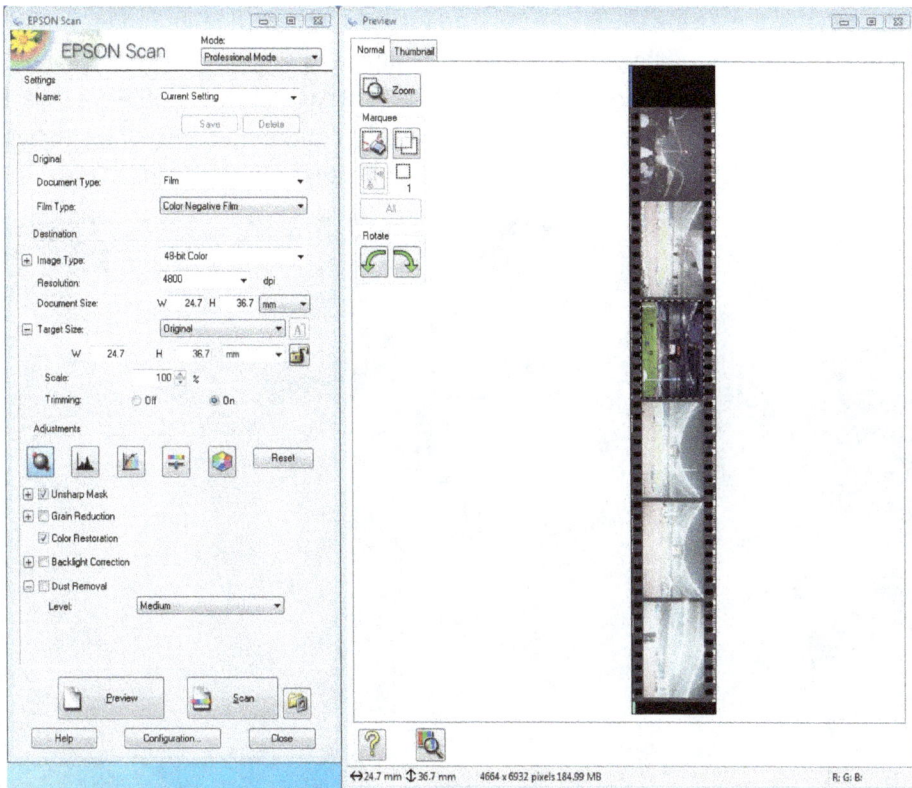

Picture 10. By selecting a single frame, the filters now give the correct colors. As in all 126 films, one has to pick 2 consecutive frames together, not necessarily the first two, but for example 3 and 4 together, or even do a partial scan, the first three and then the rest for correct color rendering.

Picture 11. Detail of a negative without frame selection

My finding is that either using the Full Auto Scan future through the film holder for 135 film, or cleaning the glass again, fixing the negative with tape and scanning in Professional Mode with "Normal" preview, there is no difference in the quality of the image file created, but only a lighter one color tone, perhaps due to the fact that in the holder the negative is 3mm above the scanner surface, resulting in shading from the edges of the holder.

Picture 12. Image from scanned negative through the 135 film holder.

Picture 13. Image from scanned negative in contact with scanner glass

11. FILM 126 SCANNING - PROCEDURE, METHODS AND RESULTS

This scanner model (Epson Perfection V370 Photo) has the ability to scan negatives as we have already mentioned and has a negative film holder for 135 films.

Putting a negative from a 126 film in the holder of the 135 and selecting the Professional Mode results in the following.

There is no case working on the Full Auto Mode, since we have to choose each negative frame manually.

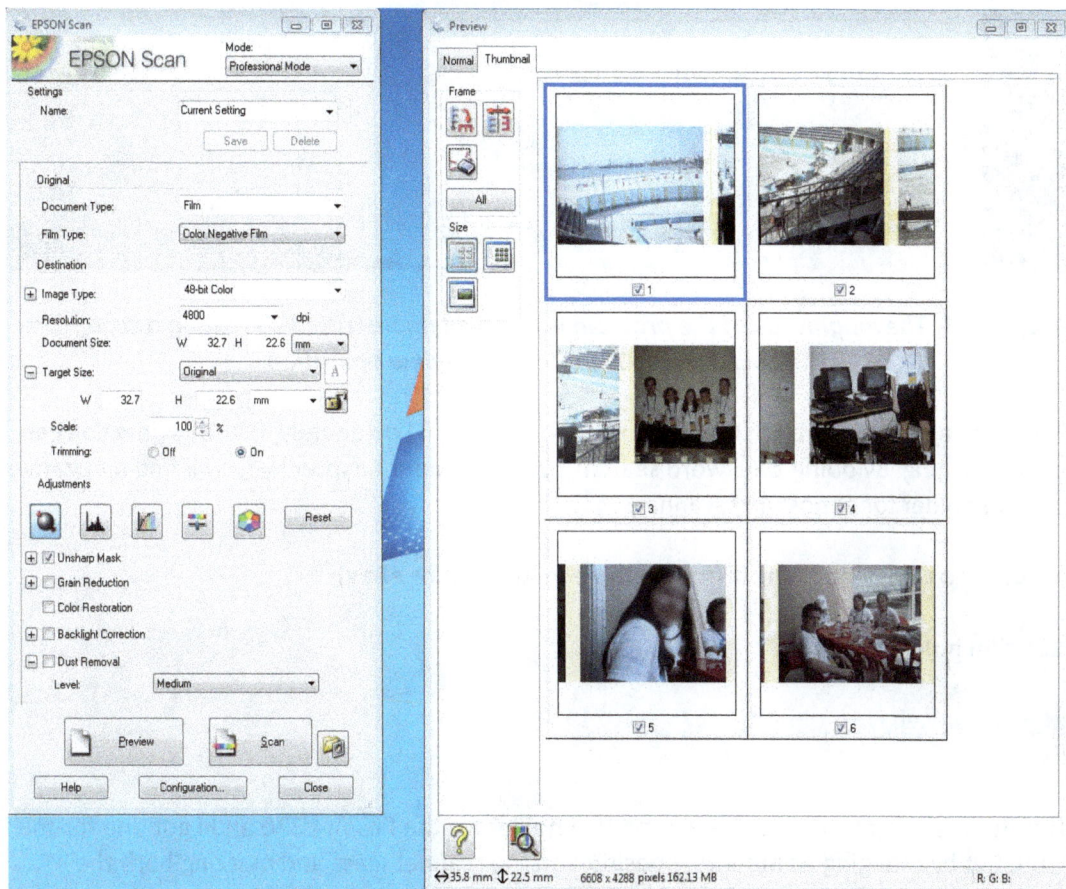

Picture 14: Placing a 126 negative in the scanner case for the 135 negative we notice that when set in Professional (manual) Mode option, the application cannot focus properly on the frame by displaying two parts of two different photos or omitting entire frames. The main thing is that due to the size difference with the 135 the negative is "cut" up and down. Characteristic example in frame 4 where both the head and the legs are cut. (p.s. photos from Olympic games "Athens 2004" test events. Faces are blurred intentionally)

Picture 15. The magnitude of the problem is clearly demonstrated by testing a scan from the holder with "Thumbnail" preview operation.

There was a serious problem here that I had to deal with. Fortunately, on eBay now you can find everything. By doing a keyword search "126 film holder adapter" you will find a negative 126 film holder for almost any scanner.

Keyword to Google it / Bing it (for example in Amazon or eBay)

"126 film holder adapter"

https://www.ebay.co.uk/itm/273767120719

Unfortunately, in this case there was no film holder for the Epson V370 and I got one for the V100. But by changing its mounting position on the scanner glass and marking both the scanner and the case it was adjusted and functioning properly.

Picture 16. Epson V100 126 film holder. To the right of the case are the markings I placed to point the exact spot that the holder must be positioned to function properly on the Epson V370

As in the 135 films, I did also two scans both from the film holder and directly from the scanner glass without noticing significant differences in quality.

In the scanner I had drew two set of markings with a black marker. One for the film holder itself when containing a negative film and one to use it as a ruler for placing the 126 films directly on the glass.

Picture 17. Placing the adapter with markings to indicate the correct spot, I positioned the film, removing it the adapter carefully.

Picture 18. Here is the 126-film positioned for scanning directly from the glass.

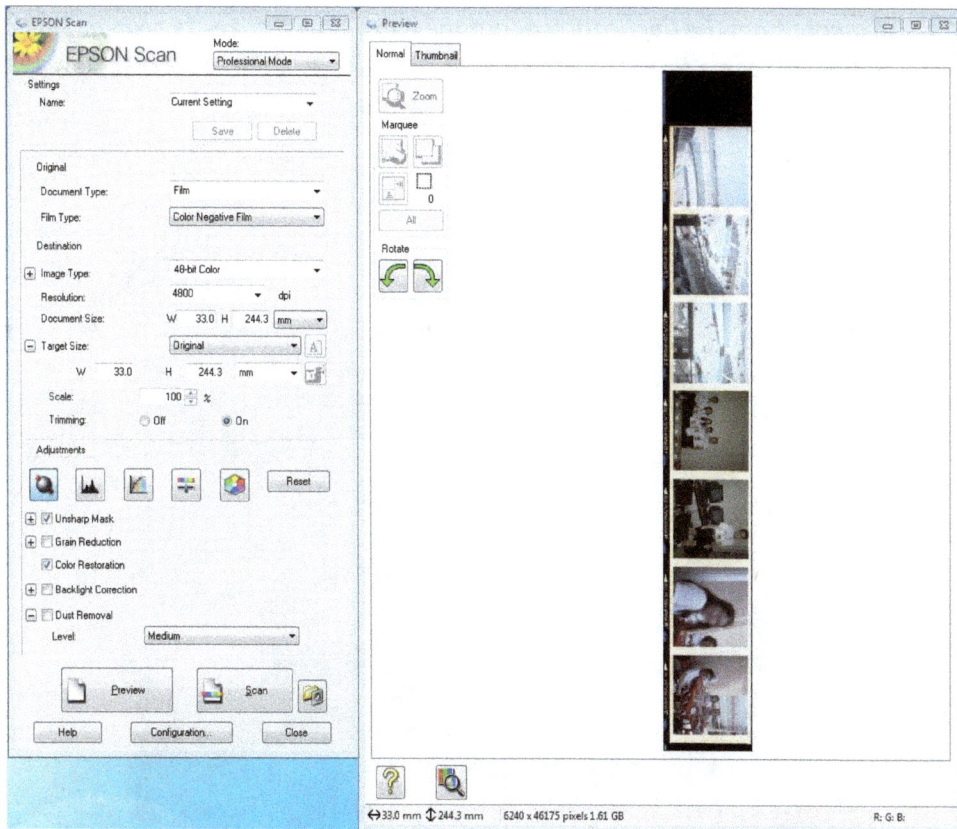

Picture 19. As with the 135 films, without selecting a specific frame the filters cannot focus on the correct colors

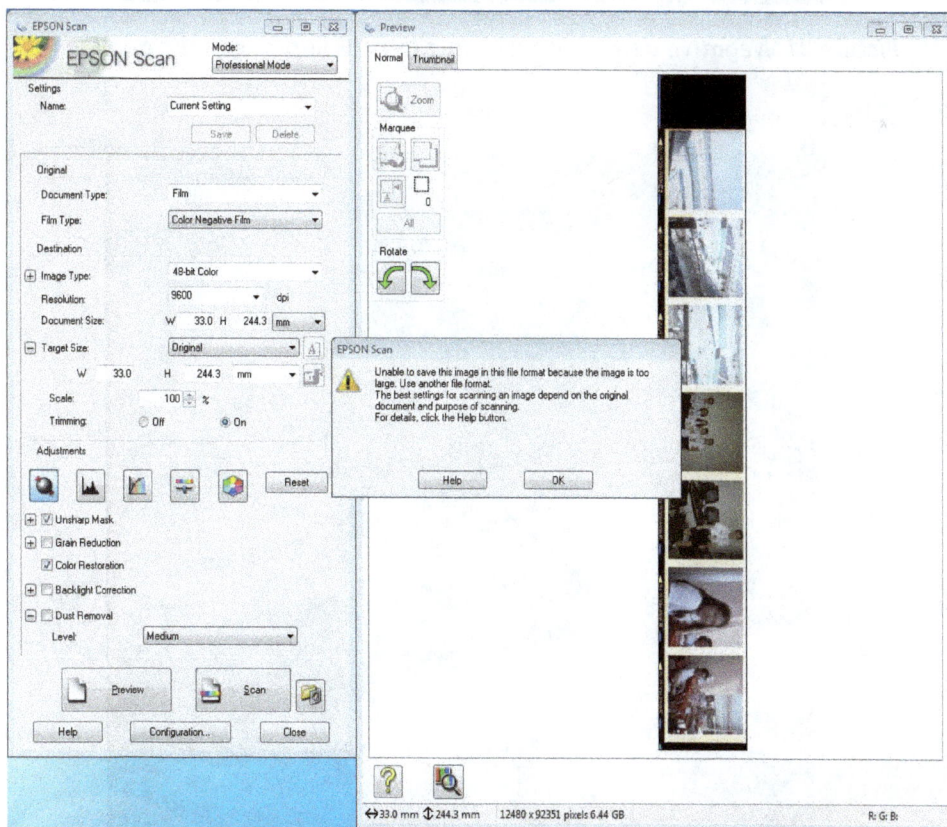

Picture 20. By selecting only one frame, the filters now give the right color. As in the 135 film it is observed that you have to select 2 consecutive frames together, not necessarily the first two, but for example 3 and 4 together or even scan partially, the first three and then the rest for color rendering correctly.

29

*Here's also a note from the application about the extra time it takes to scan at 9600dpi.
Indeed, the time to scan a frame at 4800 dpi, as we will see in the table below, is 1'.37 "
while at 9600dpi, 2 '.28 "*

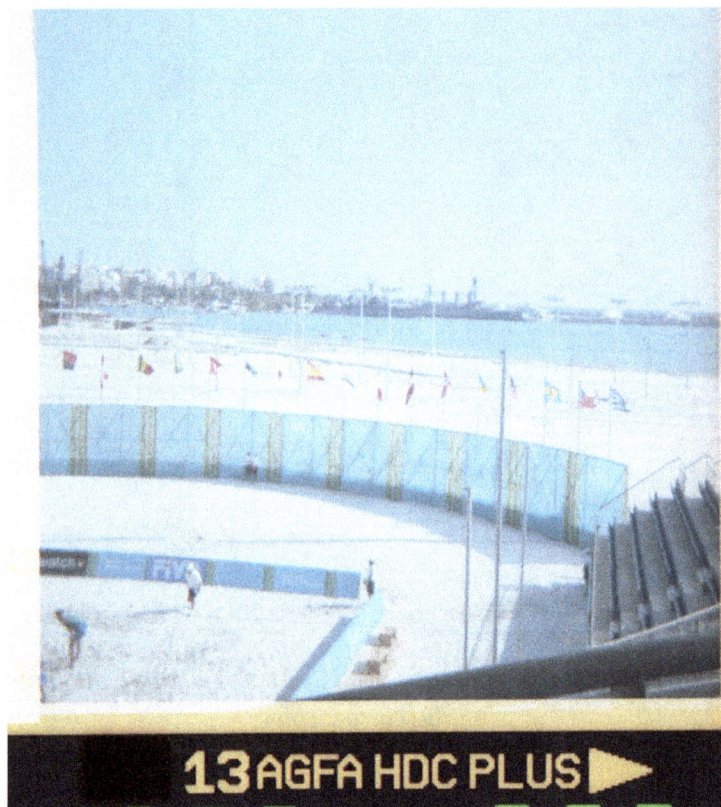

Picture 21. Negative detail without any filters or improvements applied

Picture 22. Picture from scanning 126 film through the negative holder

Picture 23. Picture from scanning 126 film negative on direct contact with the scanner glass

The scanning of a 126-negative frame at 4800 dpi produces an image with dimensions about 5467 x 5424 pixels almost twice the 4k resolution (4096 × 2160) and a relative smaller than the 8K UHD (7680 × 4320)

Picture 24. While in the 135 films negative the capture of the photograph is contained solely on the exact frame borders, in 126 films, is observed that frames are overlapping each other. According to several photographers I asked, this had to do with either the shutter speed (in particular Kodak Instamatic 126 camera)

https://en.wikipedia.org/wiki/Instamatic or the quality of the film. In other films with the same camera there is not as much overlap as in the sample above, or none at all. In a second and predominant theory it has to do with the fact that since the film had to be manually rotated to capture a photo, on the next frame, the lever that turned the film's spool had a problem, or the user didn't move properly the lever. So, there was plenty of space between the two frames. (Film Negative Overlapping)

I kept in my archive also the original scan of the whole negative (5 frames of a 126 film at 4800 dpi respectively) created a 1GB TIFF file size 5977x29483 pixels

12. FILE SIZE, SCANNING TIME, RESOLUTION, FORMAT

The following message appears when scanning above 4800dpi (in this case 9600dpi).

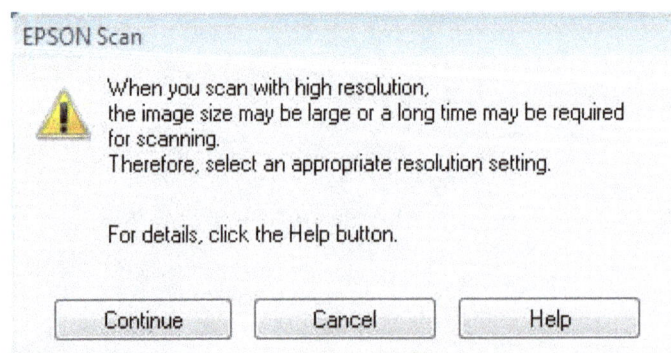

Picture 25. Warning message that the file at 9600dpi will be too large and will take a long time to scan.

Performing a scan in TIFF for example, as we have already said, since the format in its original form is uncompressed, a huge file is created. I consider it's a one-way since we definitely want the 48bit color resolution and uncompressed file so we don't have even the least loss of fidelity we would have in JPEG.

It is a practice that requires large hard disk drives but is necessary to create a complete and quality record for future generations.

Personally I did all the scans except some at 4800dpi. At 9600dpi I scanned photos of wider historical content and some extremely important family and non-family moments.

Tables with scan times depending on the resolution and file size created are following.

DPI, SCANNING TIME, RESOLUTION AND FILE SIZE IN .TIFF AND IN .JPG FOR ONE NEGATIVE FRAME FROM 135 FILM

DPI	TIME	RESOLUTION	TIFF 48bit	JPG 24bit
150	19"	205x134	169KB	7KB
300	20"	410x268	653KB	33KB
600	27"	821x536	2,53MB	98KB
1200	37"	1643x1072	10MB	320KB
2400	57"	3287x2144	40,3 MB	1,36MB
4800	1',59"	6575x4288	161MB	4,38MB
9600	3'	13151x8576	645MB	13,52MB

DPI, SCANNING TIME, RESOLUTION AND FILE SIZE IN .TIFF AND IN .JPG FOR ONE NEGATIVE FRAME FROM 126 FILM (DIMENSIONS 10X10cm)

DPI	TIME	RESOLUTION	TIFF 48bit	JPG 24bit
150	11"	168x168	172KB	8KB
300	13"	332x336	662KB	34KB
600	21"	665x672	2,56MB	87KB
1200	31"	1330x1344	10,2MB	280KB
2400	46"	2660x2688	40,9MB	1,24MB
4800	1',37"	5320x5376	163MB	4,16MB
9600	2',28"	10640x10753	654MB	13,23MB

All calculations were done with the free utility Countdown Timer and Stopwatch

https://sourceforge.net/projects/countdowntimer/

In conclusion, the scan time between 150 and 1200dpi has a difference of only 20 seconds. After 1200dpi it shoots at an incredible height, as for a 9600dpi frame we have to wait 3 minutes for the scan to be completed.

13. PHOTO SCAN (10X10, 10X15, COLOR, BLACK & WHITE AND VARIOUS SIZES)

Here the process is more or less standardized, we do not have to deal with negatives and film holders but only to place the photo in the scanner glass and make the adjustments.

Note: This particular scanner model, Epson Perfection V370 Photo has the Full Auto Mode to scan from 1 to 4 10x15 size photos automatically as well as more than 4 in the case of smaller photos.

I found this feature unsatisfactory since it did not accurately recognize the sizes and borders of the photo, cutting it from 0.2mm to 0.7mm from the edges or even focusing and scanning half the photo.

The problem was more intense in smaller size or older photos which e.g., they had a white frame and considering that he had to remove it, it also removed some of the photo.

Even with one photo at a time placed on the scanner glass, The Full Auto Mode again made cuts. So unfortunately, the photo was manually scanned at least 4 times each, as we have mentioned (2 times in JPG with and without Color Restoration reset and 2 in TIFF) resulting in additional time for the project completion.

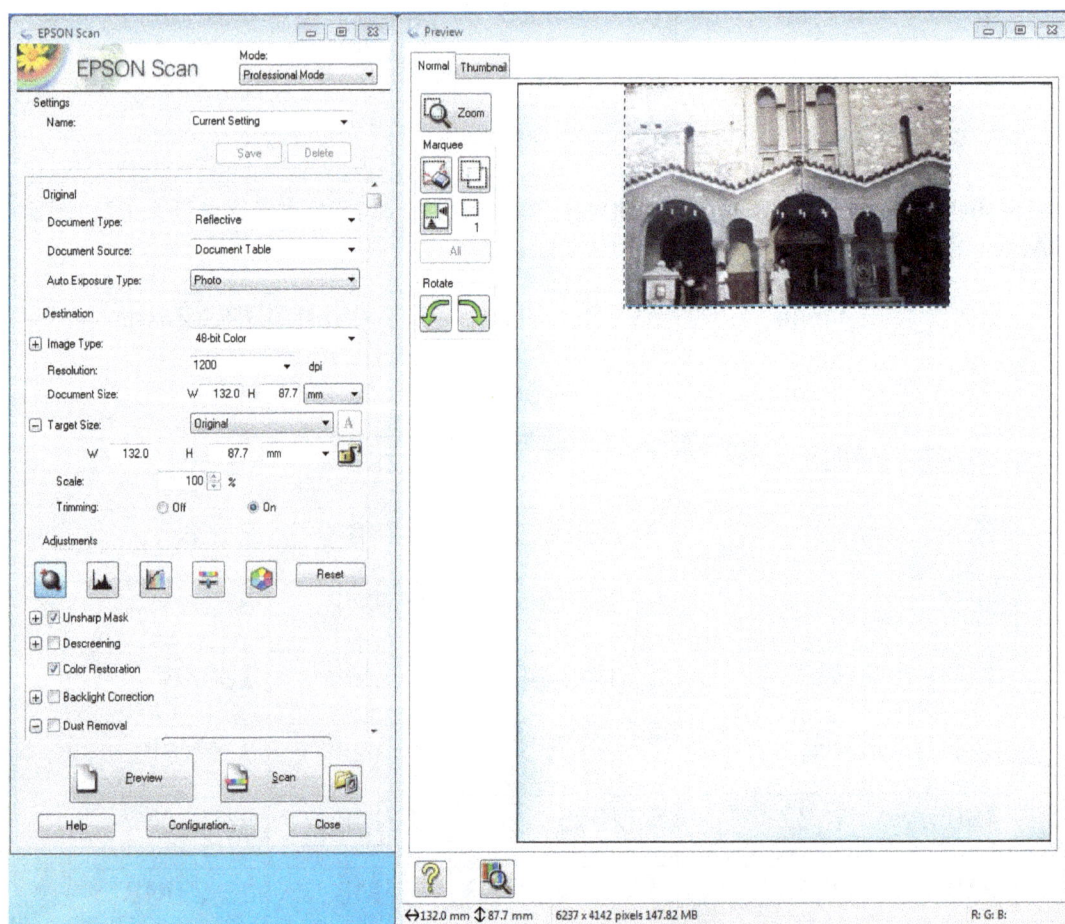

Picture 26. As I have already mentioned the photo scanning is also done in TIFF 48bit but here the scan resolution goes down to 1200dpi. In photos printed by analog display machines with a resolution of 200 or 300 dpi theoretically we will not get more detail by scanning over the 1200dpi.

Photographers told me that it makes no sense to scan the photo at high dpi, since the maximum print resolution on the paper is no more than 300-400 dpi. This is true of the second part but not the first.

Scanning at 300-400 dpi, as I describe at the beginning, we are able to create a copy of the photo and reprint it in the same dimensions with similar quality.

Scanning at 1200dpi will result in creating a larger file, simply by creating pixels, but large file resolution is a repository for future use. Especially if the original in additional 15 years of time has been further damaged when you try to scan it again then at higher resolution.

But when it comes to creating a digital archive and "Build for the future" as I described at the beginning, it is necessary to scan photos at 1200dpi if not higher.

DPI, SCANNING TIME, RESOLUTION AND FILE SIZE IN .TIFF AND IN .JPG FOR ONE NEGATIVE FRAME FROM 135 FILM (DIMENSIONS 10X15)

DPI	TIME	RESOLUTION	TIFF 48bit	JPG 24bit
150	6''	901x588	3,11MB	123KB
300	7''	1802x1177	12,44MB	395KB
600	14''	3604x2355	49,75MB	1,31MB
1200	46''	7209x4710	198,88MB	5,34MB
2400	1'57''	14419x9421	-	20,64MB
3200	5',39''	19225x12561	-	24,17MB

Above 3200dpi in a 24bit JPG format it is impossible to scan since there is a limitation by the scanner itself whose maximum useful resolution is 21000x30000 pixels and the following error message appears

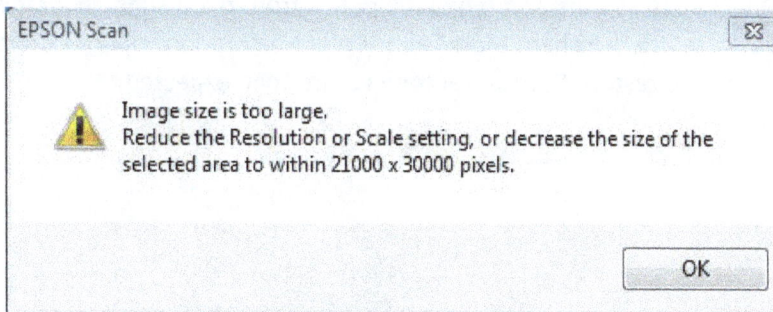

Picture 27. Error while trying to scan at 4800dpi

On scanning, at 48bit TIFF the limitation is even greater and maximum resolution is set at 10500x30000 so scanning above 1200dpi is not possible. The limitation has to do with the color depth due to the scanner limitation as well.

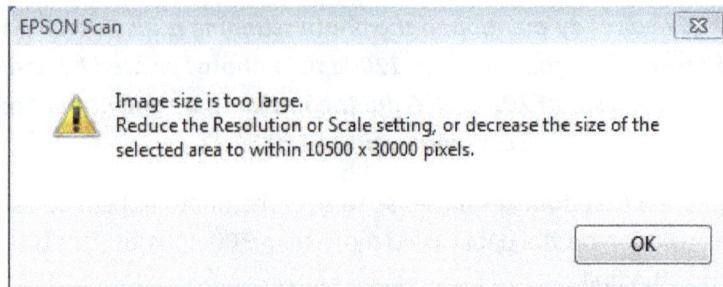

Picture 28. Error while trying to scan at 2400dpi

DPI, SCANNING TIME, RESOLUTION AND FILE SIZE IN .TIFF AND IN .JPG FOR ONE PRINTED PHOTO FROM 126 FILM (DIMENSIONS 10X10)

DPI	TIME	RESOLUTION	TIFF 48bit	JPG 24bit
150	5"	605x593	2,14MB	92KB
300	7"	1210x1186	8,42MB	309KB
600	13"	2421x2373	33,69MB	986KB
1200	46"	4843x4747	134,75MB	3,80MB
2400	2'02"	9686x9494	538,90MB	14,42MB
4800	7'27"	19372x18988	-	44,64MB

In this case, due to the smaller size of the photo we were able to scan at JPG format at 4800dpi and TIFF at 2400. Higher dpi vales showed the limitations mentioned above

14. UNSHARP MASK AND COLOR RESTORATION

In old photos the is a distinctive orange-colored patina that has covered the original colors tones. I have noticed that this happened either because of poor quality chemicals were used in the developing process, so the photo had the patina from the beginning, or it was created over time. In any case, the "Unsharp Mask" and "Color Restoration" options drastically enhance the photo and restore the natural colors more than expected.

Example 1: Photo without (Picture 29, up) and with Color Restoration (Picture 30, downκάτω)

In a different shade patina again, we notice the drastic correction made by the Color Restoration

Example 2: Photo without (Picture 31, up) and with Color Restoration (Picture 32, down)

As with the negatives, I have created digital files in four variants for each photo, two for TIFF with and without Color Restoration and two for JPG

The 126 films were developed using Kodak's C-41 processing method, which has created.

https://en.wikipedia.org/wiki/C-41_process

The quality of appearance, however, had to do with the quality of chemicals and the quality of the developing equipment. An old photographer confirmed to me that the orange patina in the 126 films (which didn't exist in all) had to do with the above factors and it was created during development.

Since most of the negatives I had worked with were 126, I made several comparisons to the same type of film over the same time period that developed in different laboratories. In others there was orange patina, even scratches and fingerprints, and in others the quality was so high that if the subject or landscape had not changed drastically, with minimal editing you could "pass" the photo that was taken today with digital camera.

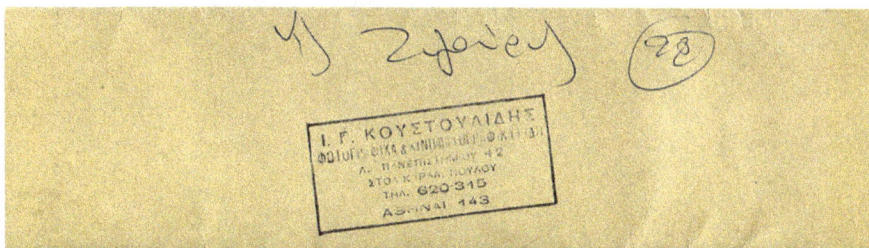

Picture 33. I would like to pay tribute even long after death to the photographic studio "Koustoulidis" 42 Panepistimiou St. Karalopoulou Gallery. In this gallery were based some of Athens' oldest photography studio and shops. By far the best developed 126 film and printed photos of the time. There are still photography shops in the gallery today.

Of course, if we go into the process of comparing the quality of a photo scanned by negative 126 and 135 film, with one taken with a modern camera (with telephoto lenses etc.) and modern printing machines (and of course much less aged by time), if we had some photos from 126 film that were looking as if they were taken today, in 135 films the same phenomenon is impressive.

In black and white photos, I found that scanning to 8, 16 bits gray or black and white adjusted the original color shades in the photo, either with or without Color Restoration.

So, I chose to scan the black and white photo with 48bit Color setting. The result is shown below.

Example 3: Black and White photo scanned without Color Restoration (Picture 34, up) and with Color Restoration (Picture 35, down)

Another remark worth noting is that in the case of converting the produced scanned image without Color Restoration to grayscale the result was a version of it, close to the one scanned without Color Restoration but with color differences. Therefore, I find that scanning in 8 or 16 bit gray or grayscale the discard of color information is detrimental to the color quality and fidelity of the original photograph and could only be used for artistic creations and illustrations only and not for the creation of a digital archive.

Contemporary photographs over the last 10 years of film use (1996-2006) have shown that Color Restoration will either not improve the image or change the color shades to worst.

Example 4: Photo without (Picture 36, up) and with Color Restoration (Picture 37, down).
We notice an intense variation and color overtones

In the above photo, initially assuming the scanner cover had not closed properly or the software might have stuck, I scanned the same photo over 5 times by taking it out and repositioning it into the glass. Then a horizontal line of light blue at the top of the photograph began to appear on the scan, which could not be removed.

I reinstalled the program, restarted the computer, and cleaned the glass without any improvement. Searching for the problem on a knowledge base, and scanner forums, on the one hand some returned the scanner as faulty to the company and thereby solved the problem, on the other hand the problem was based on the dust accumulating in the scanner corners where there are specific recesses which perform calibration on the scanner.

Although I cleaned the glass with an anti-static cloth and regularly with special wipes before each scan, however, the dust in the corners required special care to remove it.

https://files.support.epson.com/htmldocs/prv37_/prv37_ug/html/maint_1.htm#S-01100-00100

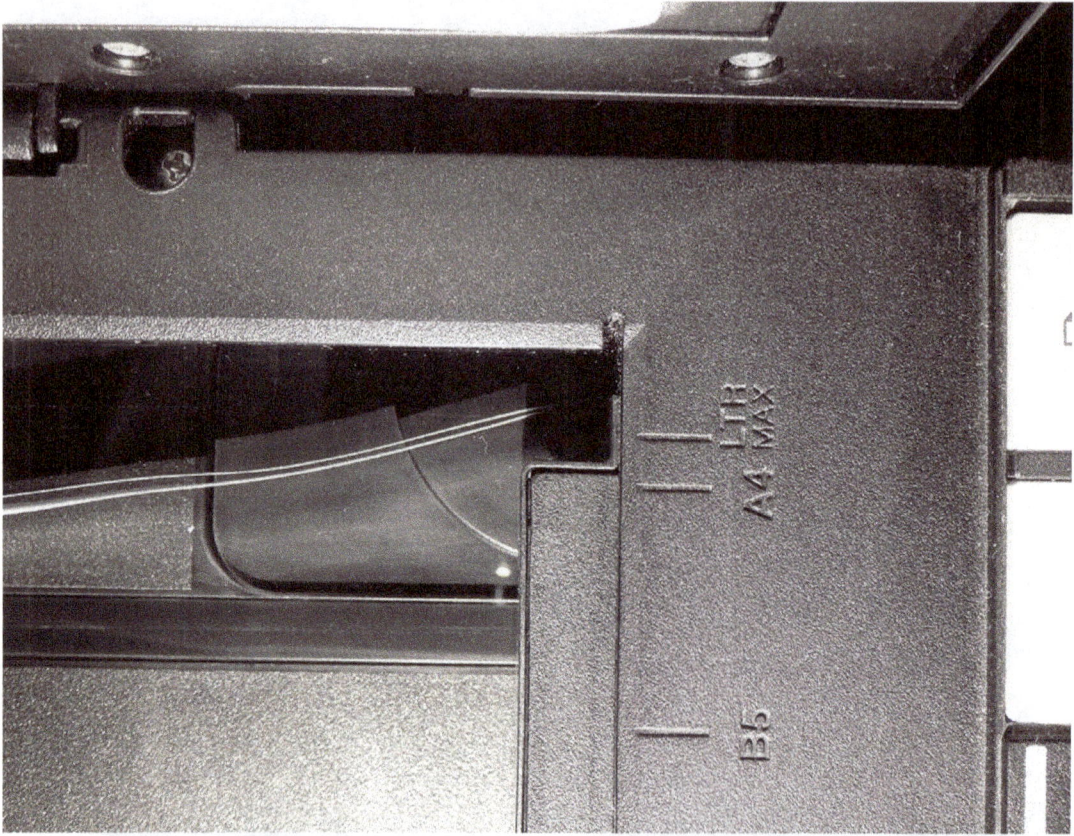

Pictures from the scanner's calibration angles where the dust is accumulated. This was the reason for the horizontal bar at the top of the photo. (Picture 38 up, Picture 39 down).

To conclude, with these procedures and methodology, a whole lost world appeared in front of me, including photos that were lost and I didn't know they exist, reprinting them from digitized negatives, loved ones who had left many years ago, moments, events, situations, toys that I had when I was a child and completely forgotten, and lots of details that looked faded or small in size in existing printed photos.

15. SCANNING 126 SLIDES

I will devote some time here to analyze the process of scanning 126 films. The slides, like the films, are available in 135 and 126 sizes. The 126 slides have exactly the same problem with films of the same type, since when placing them in the slide holder of the scanner, which is for 135 only, there is a cut at the top and bottom of the frame. Unfortunately, in this case there was no adapter available as with the films.

Scanning the Slides directly from the glass in this case was the only solution. There was not enough material except for a set of 15 Slides, but I noticed that there was no difference in the quality of the digital file compared with a well-preserved 126 film.

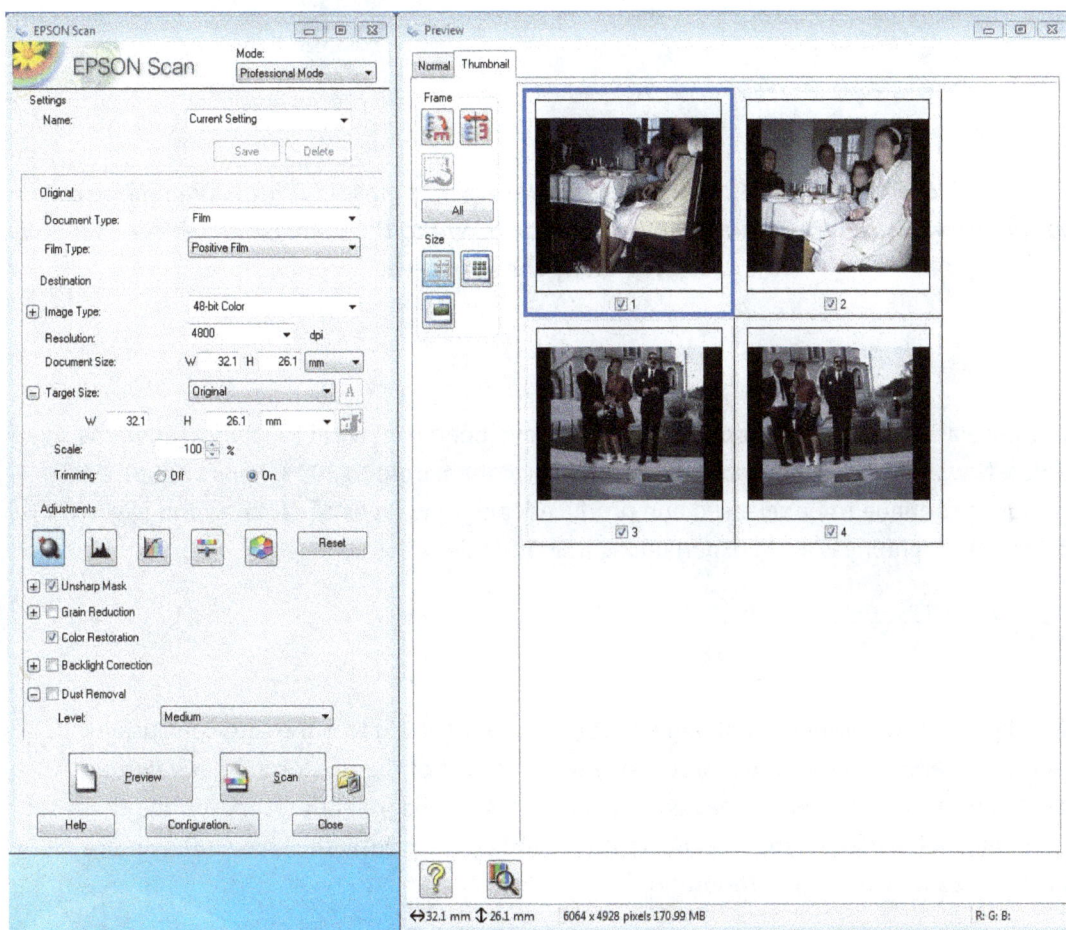

Picture 40. Scanning 126 Slides mounted on the 135-scanner case on Professional (automatic) mode. The cut at the top and bottom of the frame is evident. (p.s. Faces are blurred intentionally)

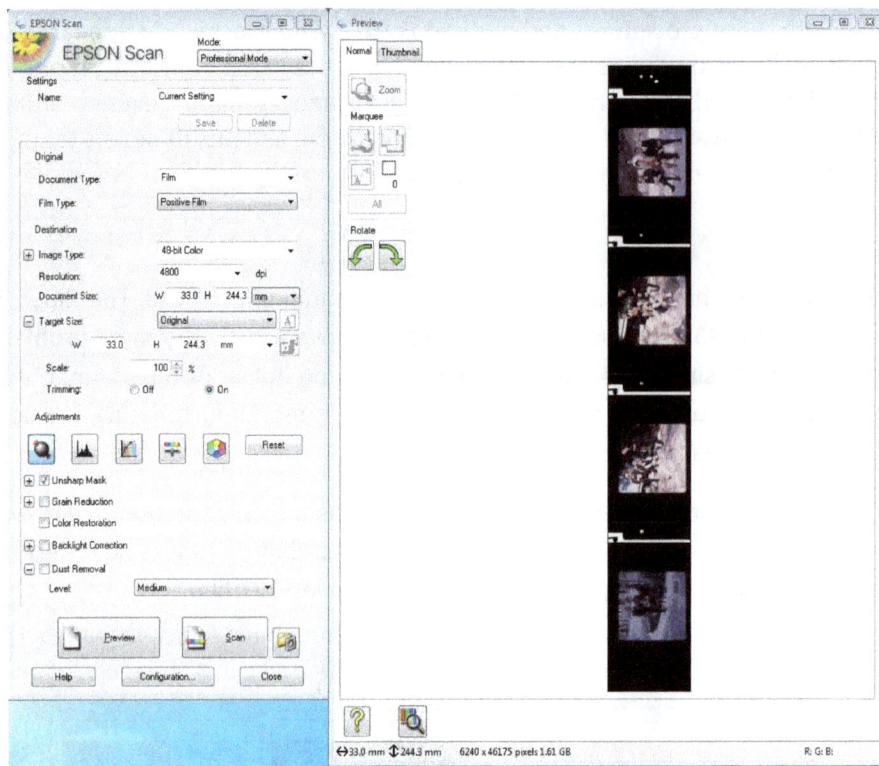

Picture 41. Scanning Slides 126 directly from the scanner glass in Professional mode but in normal preview (not thumbnail. The frame appears without cropping and we can manually select exactly the scan area.

16. SCANNING POLAROID PHOTOS

In Greece at least, the instant photos we may have been in general timely placed in the 1980s. Nowadays though, despite the bankruptcy of Polaroid to 2008, films about these machines continue to be released and produced. and new types of cameras and film, as instant photography is again experiencing a small-scale reboot.

https://en.wikipedia.org/wiki/Instant_camera

Although I also did not have enough Polaroid photos (just 20) to draw safe conclusions, it seems that although they are stored along with the rest of the photos in relatively good conditions, though not ideal, they do not have the same degree of preservation as the rest material. Their surface is much more sensitive and consequently they have many more scratches as well as color deterioration.

Speaking with photographers in general, everyone concludes that the Polaroid's biggest enemy is light and that they were not intended for archiving but for giving it to someone at the same time and so their durability is clearly less.

44

Picture 42. Instant photo (Polaroid) of 1981 scanned with the same parameters as the rest of the photos but clearly of lesser quality.

17. RESISTANCE TO TIME OF AN UNDEVELOPED 135 FILM

To sum up with the photos, let's see how long an undeveloped 135 film can withstand. This film was placed on the Canon Prima Super 105u in June 2007 without being used (the last film I sent for development with this camera was in 2006)

I had taken one photo in 2014 and two more in the summer of 2019, leaving 33 poses still available, all of which I took in December 2019 and gave it for development.

From internet sources research, there are different display methods than the usual C-41 procedure

https://en.wikipedia.org/wiki/C-41_process

Special development centers for old films that claim they can achieve very good results. Everyone agrees that the film will be distorted, resulting in fading (and therefore the developer should pay close attention to the color analyzer, as it may consider the frame to be empty and not print the photo while exists and it will just be very faded) and probably will appear an intense magenta shading depending on the type and quality of the film.

In this particular case the film was a Kodak Gold. Let's see the result.

Only 5 photos were printed from the developer. The rest were either very faded and the machine did not detect them or did not notice them.

Putting the 135-film negative in the scanner's film holder, it was possible to see all 36 photos.

Picture 43. Photo from a 135-film developed after 10 years. There is an intense blue shade in all photos.

Picture 44. The same photo with the Color Restoration. There is no real improvement. Although the photo has been lightened a little, the shades of blue remain. As we have already said in more recent films and photos, Color Correction does not have the desired results.

18. RESISTANCE TO TIME OF AN UNDEVELOPED 126 FILM

In this case we had a Kodak 126 film taken with the Kodak Instamatic 133X in April 1986 and developed in October 1990. I didn't give it for development personally, but having in my possession the negatives and the printed photos I can attest to two issues that internet sources cited. The magenta shade and the fact that the film was starting to fade from the edges inward.

Picture 45. Photo from 126 film, developed after 4 years. There is an intense magenta shade and fade from the edges inward in all photos.

Picture 46. Here the Color Restoration option restored a portion of the original colors at least in the center of the photo.

CHAPTER THREE

DOCUMENT SCANNING

19. PROCEDURE, RESOLUTION, LOSSY FILE COMPRESSION

More or less, we have all scanned at least one document in our lives. Many, depending on the all-in-one printer or scanner (few people have a separate scanner) automatically use the Scan and Mail option - and since the process is done automatically, they have not been substantially involved with all the processes and parameters available behind a simple scan. So, as we have talked extensively about digitizing photos for archival purposes, we will also see the process of scanning documents for the same purpose. Here things are much easier since we are not dealing with negatives, long scan times and with multiple scans in JPG and TIFF.

We set the scanner to Document and scanning resolution to at least 300 dpi

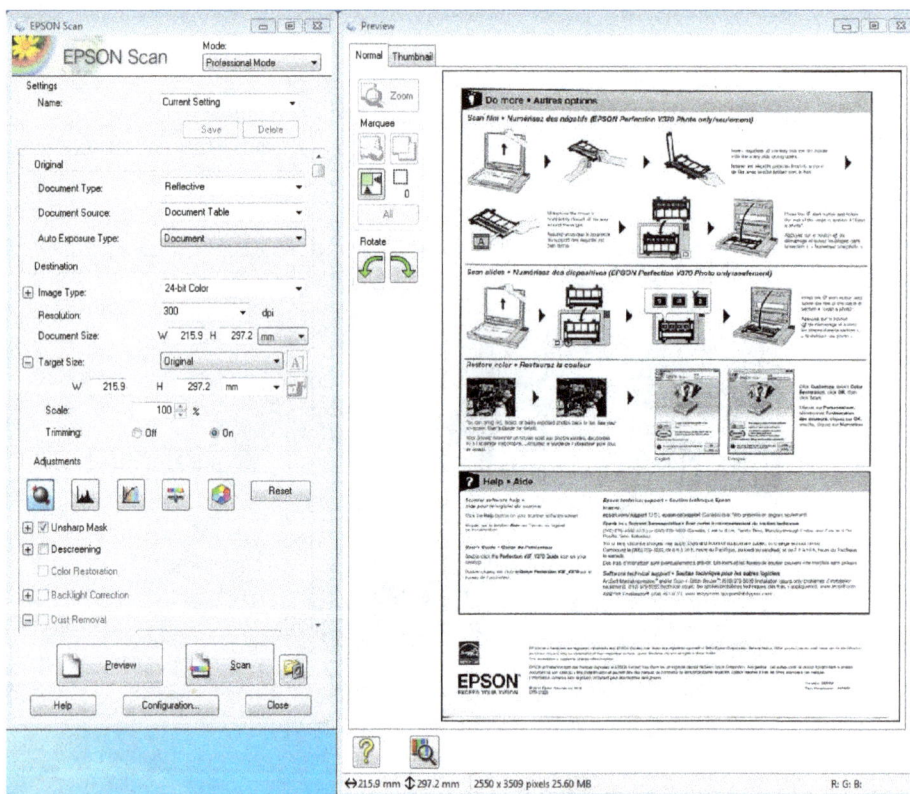

Picture 47. Document scanning. In the specific case of the scanner's instruction page, although coming from a black and white printer was set to scanned in color mode.

I then proceeded to successive scans with different settings and analyzes to identify discrepancies and compare results.

I performed 9 scans at 50 to 1200 dpi resolution. Satisfactory sharpness of the document is seen at 150dpi and above, while very small details (small fonts, footnotes, etc.) are sufficiently sharp at 300 dpi or more.

As an example, scanning the tax clearance from taxisnet (The Greek IRS service), which contains characters in very small fonts, is not readable below 300 dpi, achieving quality similar to that of the original pdf file, which automatically taxisnet generates at 400 dpi and up.

Even the Declaration of Independence of the United States of America measures 3765x4578, equivalent to about 420 dpi, of course with a scanner that had a much higher digital sensor but not much larger dpi.

https://www.archives.gov/founding-docs/downloads

https://www.archives.gov/files/founding-docs/downloads/Declaration_Pg1of1_AC.jpg?download=true&filename=Declaration-of%20Independence.jpeg

I personally used 1200dpi scanning with TIFF 48bit on only two occasions, first on a King's Otto royal decree of "awarding a lieutenant general rank" and second, on a handwritten order by General Nikolaos Plastiras in Asia Minor.

DPI, SCANNING TIME, RESOLUTION AND FILE SIZE IN .JPG 24 BIT .TIFF 24 BIT AND TIFF 48 BIT OF AN A4 PAGE

DPI	TIME	RESOLUTION	JPG 24bit	TIFF 24bit	TIFF 48bit
50	9"	425x584	152KB	737KB	1,465MB
72	10"	612x842	282KB	1,521MB	3,032MB
96	11"	816x1123	479KB	2,697MB	5,387MB
150	12"	1275x1754	1,122MB	6,568MB	13,127MB
200	13"	1700x2339	2,092MB	11,677MB	23,326MB
300	15"	2250x3509	4,460MB	26,251MB	52,466MB
400	24"	3400x4679	7,952MB	46,653MB	93,260MB
600	35"	5100x7019	17,287MB	104,938MB	209,811MB
1200	2',05"	10200x14039	61,980MB	419,644MB	839,168MB

In this table we observe a significant increase in scanning time after 300 dpi and extremely high resolution and file size (0.8GB for an A4 page in TIFF 48bit format)

The large size of the files is mainly due to the fact that I have set the JPG compression to 1 (as we have already mentioned JPG implements a lossy compression which results in the loss of information from the file)

By setting the scanner also to gray or black and white mode instead of color scanning mode, it reduces the size of the output file but not to the standard sizes produced in Full Auto Mode or in scanning and mailing mode (Scan and Email)

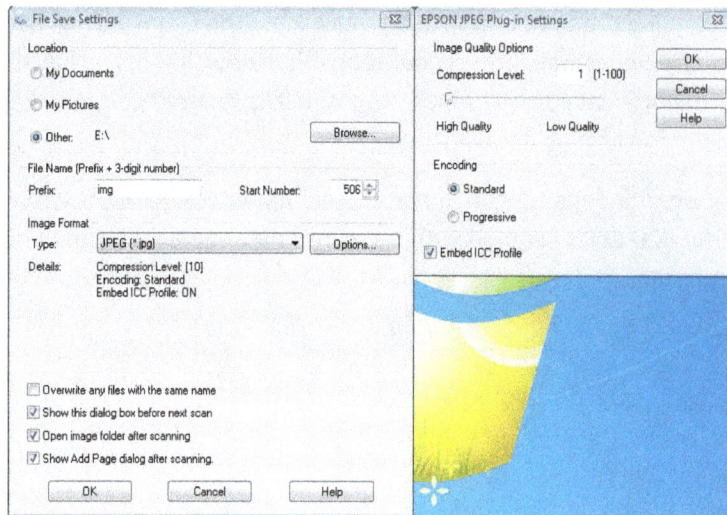

Picture 48. Compression in the smallest possible setting (in this case in 1) is characterized as excessive by photo professionals. A photographer has told me that even for photos of weddings and christenings that has covered with a DSLR camera has the compression set to 90 (compared to the scale in the photo above it is like moving the pointer to 10)

Immediately the file size of an A4 page scanned at 300 dpi, JPEG 24bit while compressing at 1 is 5,224MB with compression at 10, the size of the same file drops to 2,155MB.

So, by reducing the compression a little bit more, A4 files are created at 300 dpi, 200 to 400KB in size, which are very easy to send by email, maintaining a sufficient quality.

CHAPTER FOUR

ARCHIVAL, DOCUMENTATION AND ARCHIVAL OF DIGITIZED FILES

20. ARCHIVAL FOLDER STRUCTURE - DOCUMENTATION

In this chapter I considered it appropriate not to resort to standard archiving solutions and to pursue my own approach to the matter.

The digitized material had to be placed in continuity and relevance folders.

The first level folder is the following

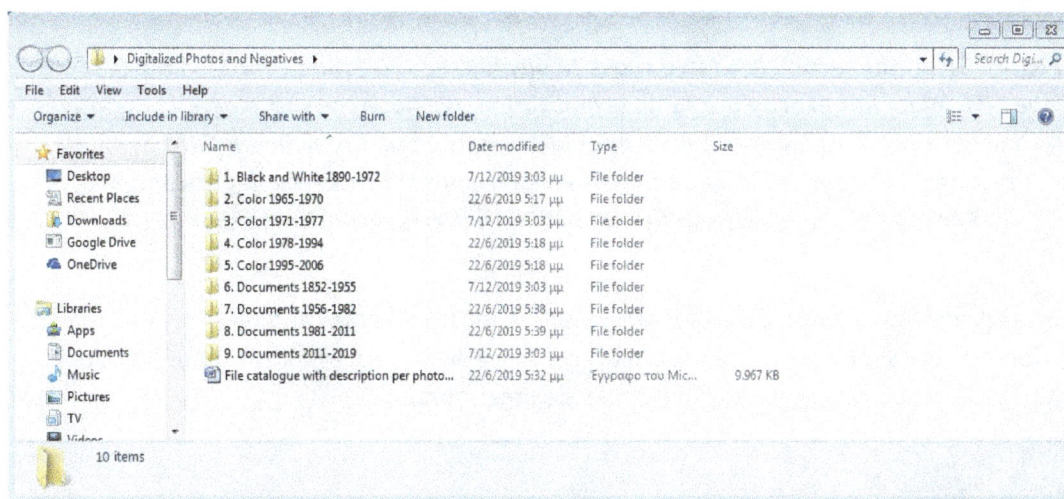

Picture 49. Folders 1 through 5 contain the photos (the photos stop in 2006 where the last 135 film was shot) and from 6 through 9 documents with specific criteria that we will analyze below.

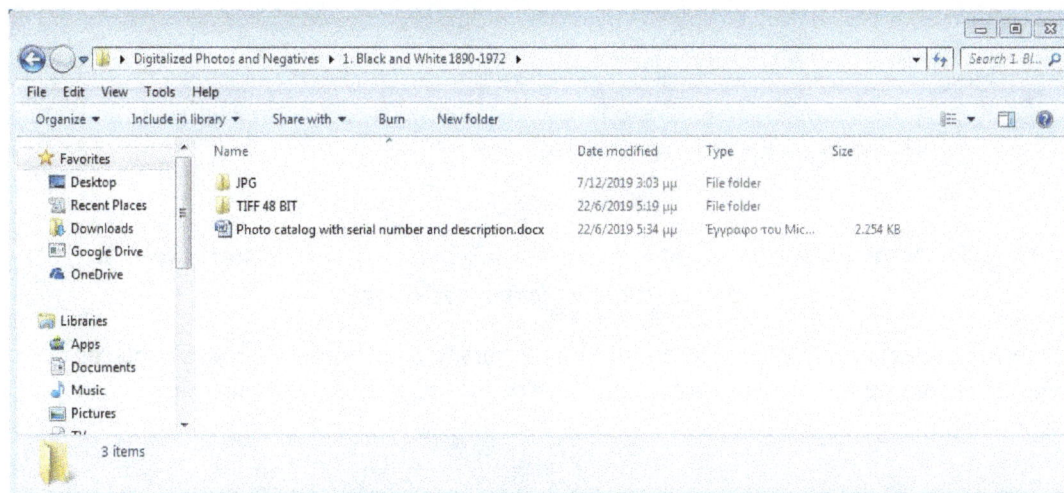

Picture 50. As for folder 1 where the black and white photos are located, at the first folder level, we have two JPG and TIFF 48 BIT subfolders. Here is also a list of descriptions and information that may be available for each photo (place taken, time, persons illustrated, historical information, etc.) with a serial number per photo.

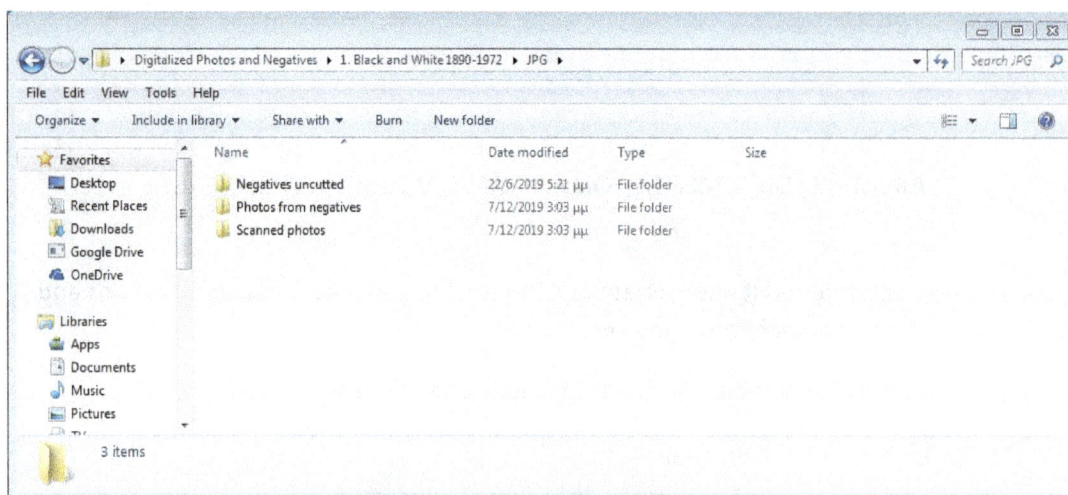

Picture 51. At the second level (we chose to display the JPG folder simply as the first one, the TIFF folder has exactly the same organization) we have the subfolders 1) Negatives uncutted (where as we have already said are located all the scanned films, without procession in usually 5-6 large files 2) Photographs cut from the negatives and 3) Photographs printed from the same film that existed and were digitalized.

In black and white photos, the negatives were at most 15 frames and there was no reason for a special subfolder, so they are placed all together (in color photos there is another folder and file organization)

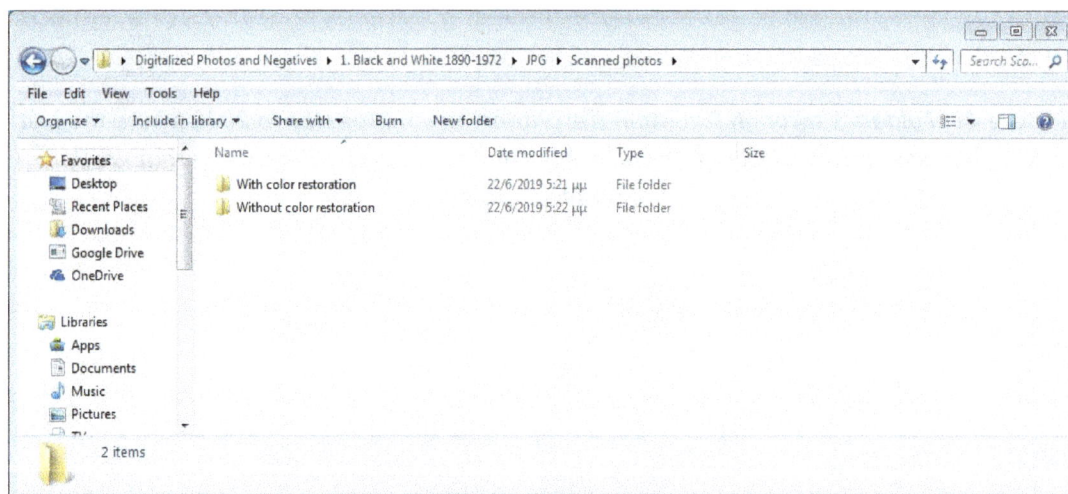

Picture 52. At the third level we have two more subfolders 1) Color restoration and 2) No color restoration (explained above)

Some 6 decades ago there were street photographers who took photos in public places, taverns, etc. you could have these photos some days later as the developing was time consuming.

The photographers did not keep the negatives which were discarded.

Closer to our times again, but before the digital age, the developing was much faster and you could have the photos during the event but the negatives were still not maintained.

Today photographers in clubs, malls, birthday parties etc. do not preserve the digital files from the camera card (the photos are now developed within half an hour so you have them directly in your hands) but even if they keep them, they refuse to hand them over to you.

The same goes for wedding and christening photographers where you can never own the digital files which are kept by the photographer.

Here I would like to mention that since May 25, 2018, the implementation of the General Data Protection Regulation (GDPR) has created a huge legal gap in how a photographer is legalized to keep a digital record of Marriage, Baptism, Event etc. virtually without the consent of the person concerned.

In the years to come, there will be a major issue with this.

Coming back to the subject, even if someone had taken pictures with their own camera, they rarely reprinted and in the vast majority of cases the negatives were thrown away.

Now we go to the Color Photos and open Folder 3 (Color 1971-1977)

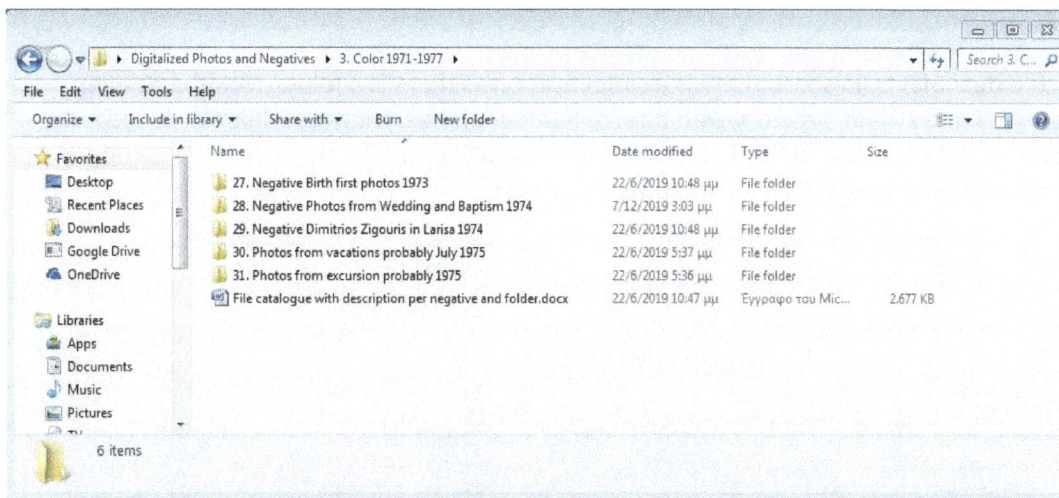

Picture 53. Here we observe the variation of the folder organization for color photos compared to those for black and white. There are folders with a negative film number, with a serial number (proportionally to 120 films there were film negatives complete or fragmented for 89), photo folders (without negatives) and a file catalogue with a photo description per negative and folder, as in the black and white photos folder.

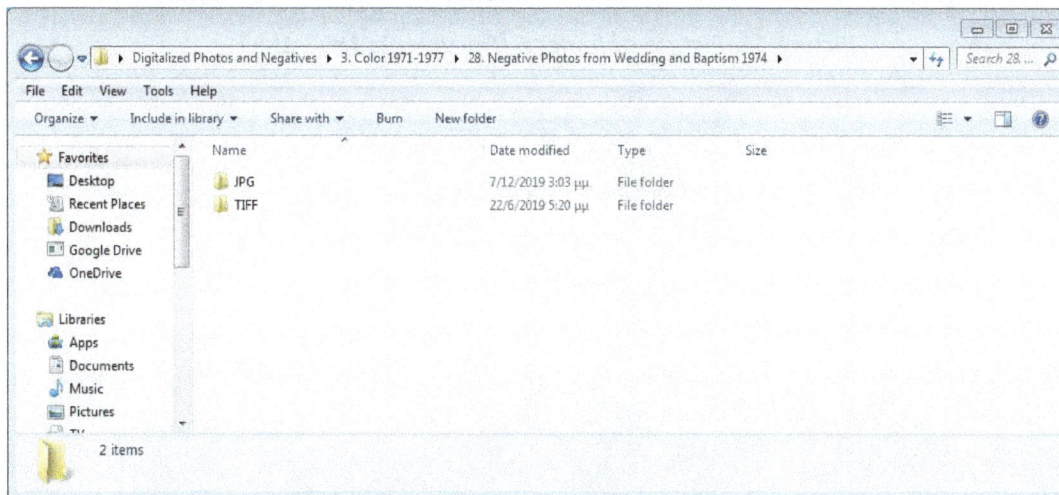

Picture 54. Going to folder 28, on the second level, we see here again two subfolders with JPG and TIFF versions of the photos.

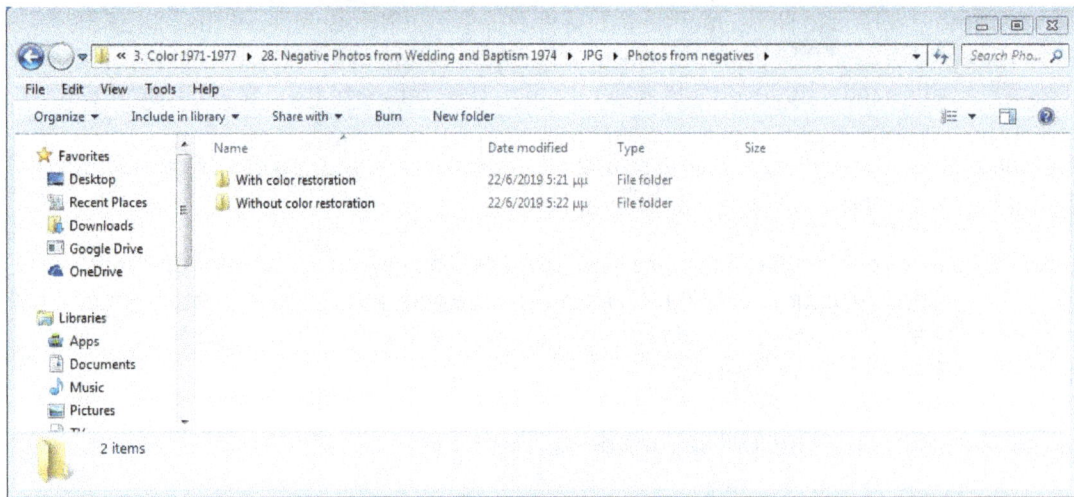

Picture 55. Opening the JPG folder, at the third level we have two more subfolders where the photos are with 1) Color restoration and 2) Without color restoration, as in black and white folder.

In the documents, in short, there is a simplification as there is a folder with themes per category and a main directory with a serial number and description, while at the second level we only have a subfolder of all documents in JPG format without Color Restoration (except in two cases in TIFF, as I mentioned above)

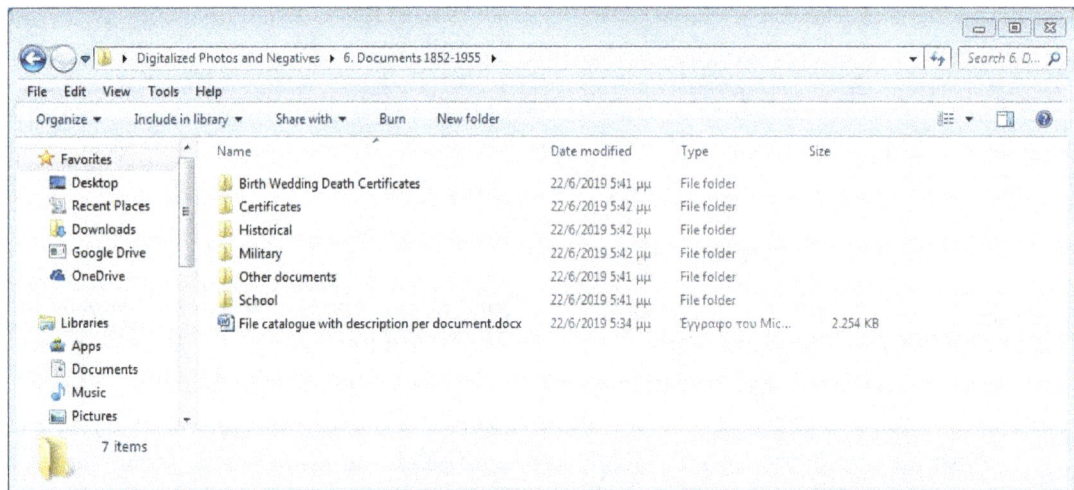

Picture 56. Picture of folder 6 (Documents 1852-1955)

20.1 FILE SECURITY AND ENCRYPTION

A person asked once: "What kind of encryption should I use in order to have my files protected in case law enforcement agencies come into my house and confiscate my computers for investigation?"

The answer is simple. You should not break the law in any way so the law enforcement agencies will not have a reason to confiscate your computers in the first place.

Apart from legal investigation, theft and sometimes non authorized access from friends and family can occur in your personal data.

For such cases is recommended, for Windows computers to always use Bitlocker. (Always print the recovery key and keep it in a different place)

https://en.wikipedia.org/wiki/BitLocker

For removable devices I recommend the WD My Book or WD Passport hard drives that coming with the WD Security technology that supports 256-bit AES hardware encryption.

https://support-en.wd.com/app/answers/detailweb/a_id/50390/~/wd-security-password-protection-for-wd-drives-guided-assist

For USB flash drivers recommended is the Sandisk Secure Access 3.0

https://www.partitionwizard.com/partitionmanager/sandisk-secure-access.html

All above methods are also available for Mac computers.

More than one encryption method can be applied but be cautions with incompatibilities that might occur.

As an alternative to those is Veracrypt, a free open source disk encryption software for Windows, Mac OSX and Linux.

https://www.veracrypt.fr/en/Home.html

Take into account that forgetting or losing the encryption password means losing forever your files.

Although the 256-bit encryption is considered to be unbreakable using current technology and computer power and theoretically, it would take billions of years for even the most powerful computers to brute force a 256-bit encryption key, yet nothing is totally safe.

A software or hardware glitch attack can bypass the security key and your data can be compromised.

Choose your course of action wisely in every aspect. (That might sound like an ancient Greek quote but it represents the truth).

21. CLASSIFICATION ISSUES

Here, because I did not want to interrupt the above analysis of the archiving and documentation process, I would like to make a citation reference.

The files were named according to the serial number of the negative frame where available.

Picture 57. Here we see the underside of a 126-film negative. It is numbered from 1 to 6. Therefore, the picture from frame 1 of negative number 28 was named 28.P1.jpg. P corresponds to the first letter of the word Pose, e.g., "strike a pose to photograph you". If the negative was not saved in full, e.g., all 24 frames, only the frames that exist were numbered of course.

In scanned printed photos for which there was no frame available from the negative the files were named for example 28.PX1.jpg, where X corresponds to an unknown number of frames. From the sequence and relevance of the photos we could try to give a number but I did not do so to avoid inconsistencies.

Also, worth mentioning is a problem I encountered in photos.

I came across several photos that had been taken the same day, at the same event with different cameras, or the film of a different company, or at the same place at a different event.

In the absence of negatives, where they would help us distinguish which film they belonged the photos belong to, based on the serial number of the negatives, the poses, or the filmmaker, there was an objective difficulty in classifying the photographs.

In this case I used another method. The photos, depending on which album the space had been placed in, had a patina with yellow tones on their backs. The intensity of the color of the patina and the various distinguishing marks and numbers on the back of the printing machines made it possible to sort them.

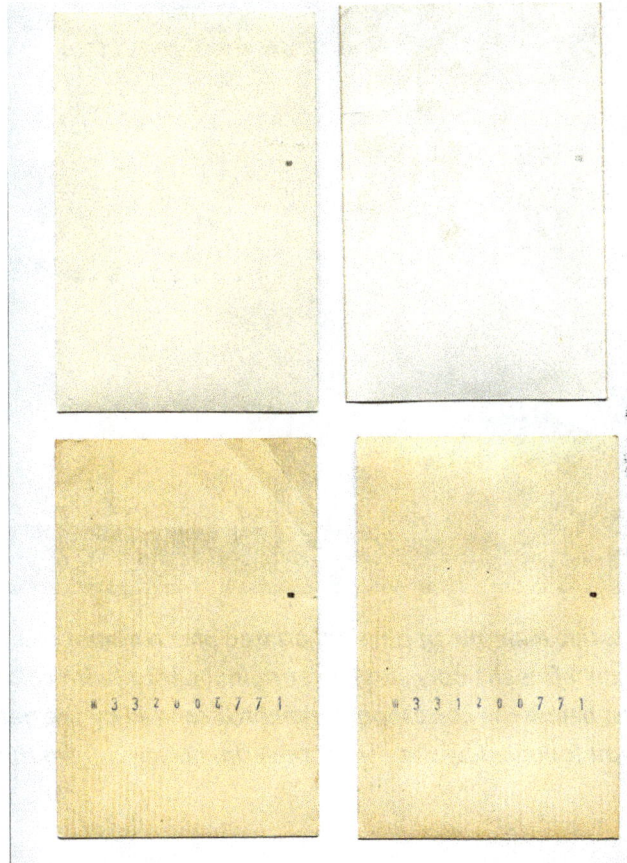

Picture 58. Four photos with the same thematic content and size where with a reference point the patina and the signs and numbers on the back, we were able to sort them.

22. RECONSTRUCTION OF A PHOTO ALBUM

The creation of digital photo albums for baptismal, wedding, etc., is now prevalent worldwide, which contradicts the so-called analogue.

To be precise the terms are incorrect since in the first case we are talking about an album that has been digitally edited and printed on special paper with various laminating and binding methods and in the second for photographs that come from a digital camera and after they are printed are placed in a simple photo album.
It is not a technically a matter of virtually digital or analogous on real terms, but of using terminology for the photographers to distinguish, mainly to their clients, the difference between the albums.

A proper rendering for the sake of differentiation would be a digitally printed and a physical album.

Without wanting to be boring, both types of albums are generally not considered digital since they are printed on paper and the only thing that can be called a digital album is to put photos from the event in sequence, in a digital photo frame or in a folder on our mobile phones, laptops, etc.

Below we will see how we recreate a 1970s photo album.

At first, I pulled off with great care the photos from the old album (the albums of that time had a certain adhesive substance to hold the photos in place that in the decades had passed, albums and photography had become one.

57

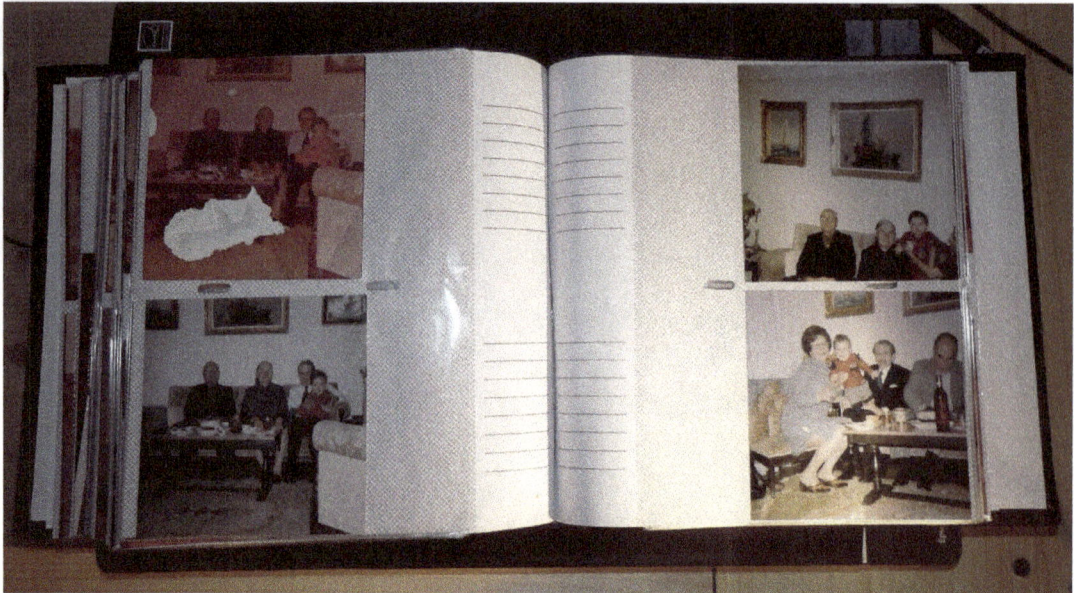

Picture 59. Representative example of physical printed photo album reconstitution. In the first position on the top left is the only surviving original photo (with color patina from the decades and torn) just below the corresponding photo scanned by the negative and printed and to the right followed by the others by serial number, from the negative.

CHAPTER FIVE

STORAGE

23. STORAGE OF NEGATIVES AND PHOTOS

Here I am referring to the storage of negatives and photos, which is not the subject of this research but nevertheless I feel that a reference needs to be made.

The negatives of at least the last 10 years I have had (1996-2006) have come mostly from the development center on polyethylene holders, which according to the general acceptance of the photographic community is the most appropriate for storing negatives since this material is proven that does not damage the film.

Of course, all other parameters (avoid sunlight, high temperature, humidity, etc.) must also be taken in mind.

The storage conditions for the negatives are the same for printed photos that should also be placed in albums and boxes that do not contain acids or PVC which are most suitable for archiving.

For more information on acid-free paper read the link below

https://en.wikipedia.org/wiki/Acid-free_paper

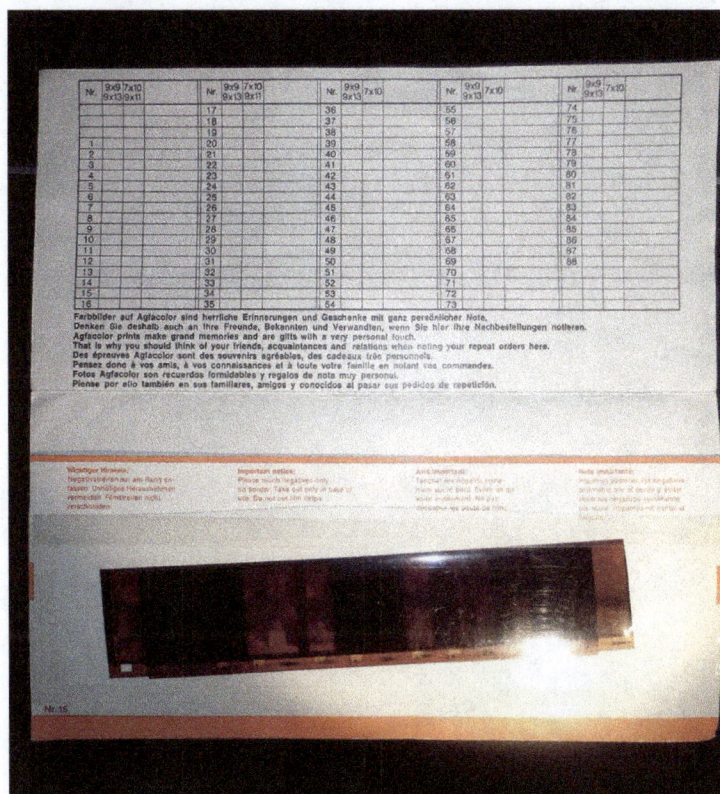

Picture 60. Negative of 1971, all negatives in one plastic holder

Picture 61. Negative of 1973 with a separate plastic holder for each negative

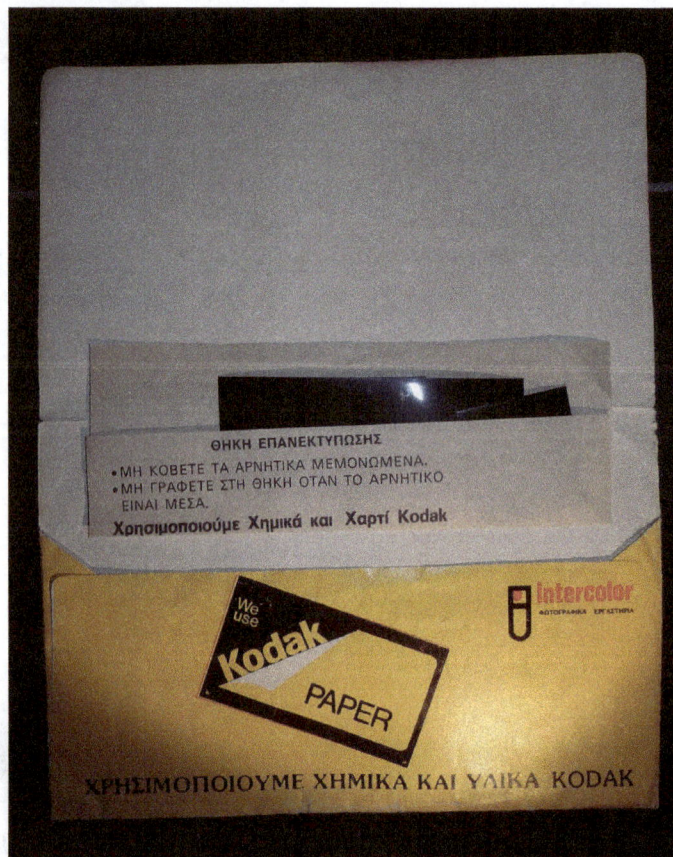

Picture 62. Negative of 1993 with all negatives together in one paper holder

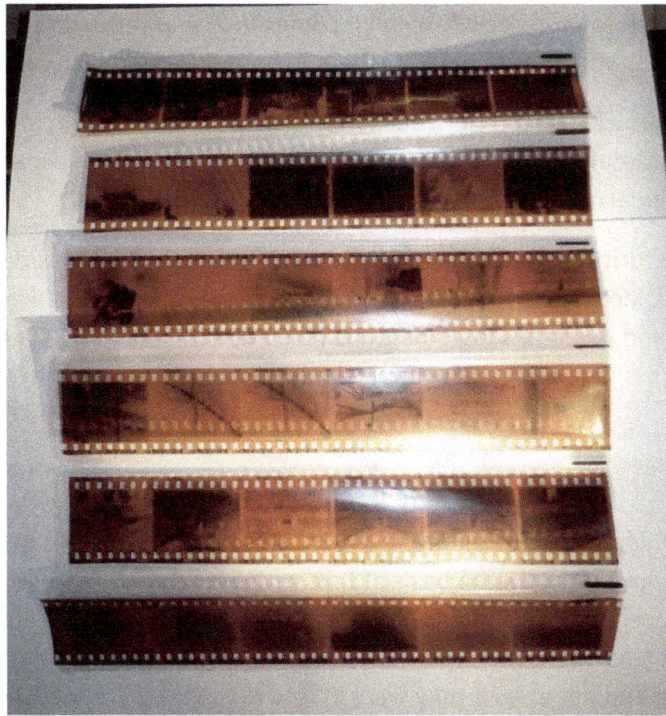

Picture 63. Negative of 2004 with polyethylene holder for each negative piece separately.

24. DATA STORAGE - CREATION OF BACKUP COPIES

So, since we have now converted all our data into digital form and archived it (see also the annex) we are going to the big issue of storage.

I constantly hear about data loss almost daily, whether this is wedding or christening photos, or of the children when they were young (the ones above, I have found to have the greatest psychological impact, then the loss of important corporate data) even from accounting and architectural offices etc.

As I have mentioned in other cases above, my purpose is not to give instructions on how NAS devices or backup programs work, but to document a proven way of safely storing data in terms of minimize close to zero a possible loss, but also in the case of interception or breach.

25. STORAGE DEVICES

Existing storage modes up to this time are as follows.

1. USB Flash Drive - easy to use, big chance of loss of device, possible damage

2. CD / DVD / BLU-RAY - no longer used by ordinary users, a great level of safety if maintained under normal conditions.

3. Internal Hard Disk - Branded hard disks as I have described can have a life span of more than 10 years. But damage is always possible.

4. External Hard Disk Drive - It can also withstand more than a decade, but statistics show more damage chance (either 3.5 or 2.5 inches), risk of falling.

5. NAS Storage - Much safer especially when it comes to 2, 4 or more disk raid arrays, a very expensive solution for home users both for the purchase and overall storage cost.

6. Cloud Storage - Security, encryption, ability to retrieve data even from previous version of the file, free and affordable solution but not for large amount of data, expensive cost for large capacities, annual or monthly subscription.

I will not analyze security in all storage modes e.g., on a digital camera card, mobile phone, or USB Flash Drive, since we consider that the above media, can only be accounted for, as a temporal storage (and the data should be transferred directly to another media) for example it is totally unreasonable to have travel photos only on camera and to use it to view them.

26. RECORDING ON CD / DVD

To begin with, I would first like to refer to a theory that has existed since the age of magnetic storage media, (floppy disks). On the basis of this, with available diskette capacities of 720kb or 1.44mb (High Density) some opted for storing collection of files e.g., 1.40MB size to use two 720kb disks instead one 1.44MB on the assumption that if one of them fails, only half the data will be lost and not all as if they were stored on a 1.44MB floppy disk

The same thing began later for hard drives (internal and external) e.g., to have the data on two 500MB drives instead of one 1GB.

Gigabytes have become Terabytes, floppy disks are no longer used for storage, hard disk drives and optical media are built with advanced technologies that guarantee a longer life but the theory continues to survive to this day.

We will deal extensively with the application of this theory in optical media.

So, if we burn a 4.7GB DVD the contents of the 6.7 700MB CDs are theoretically 6.7 times more likely to be lost.

If we do the same thing with an 8.5GB Double Layer DVD we are talking about 2 to 1 chance of losing data or if we burn 12 CDs the chances are 12 to 1.

27. RECORDING ON BLU-RAY

This is how we get to Blu-Ray which comes in 25, 50, 100 and 128 GB capacities, you will hardly find more than 25GB of storage in store and you will have to order larger capacities on e-shops.

On an experimental level, 200 and 400GB disks have been manufactured while a new laser technology promise disks up to 1TB or larger.

https://en.wikipedia.org/wiki/Blu-ray

So, you understand that based on the theory that we negotiate a simple scratch on a 4.7 GB DVD would mean X unreadable blocks of data, the same scratch on a 50 GB Blu-ray entails a loss of X by 10.6 data blocks.

The everyday use of our optical and magnetic data has proven that this theory does not apply. One could say that this is the exception, not the rule, though this proposal itself would be more or less a sophistry.

Even if as, you will see below, we have an external hard drive that has been working smoothly for 10 years, there is no reason to have our data only there (but to have multiple backups) and of course we can also send the specific disk in recycling and replace it with a new one that incorporates new data security technologies, encryption, USB 3.0 etc.

Based on my personal experience I give the following certified life spans for magnetic and optical media.

28. INDICATIVE LIFE SPANS OF MAGNETIC AND OPTICAL MEDIA

No	MEDIUM / YEAR OF CREATION (IF APPLICABLE)	YEARS WITHSTANDING
1	**3.5-inch Floppy Disk with DOS program** (Norton Commander) written in 1993, still working	30
2	**5.25-inch Floppy Disk** written in 1991, still working	32
3	**3.5-inch Floppy Disk** for booting a Windows 98 installation written in 2000, still works	23
4	CD written in 2000	23
5	**Commercial CD**	32
6	**DVD** written in 2005	18
7	**Commercial DVD**	29
8	**Blank DVD** of 2007, recorded in 2019 without any problems	16
9	**Blu-Ray** Written in 2009	14
10	**External Hard Disk Drive**, operating 2-3 hours a day since 2009	14
11	**Internal Hard Disk Drive,** operating 10 Hours Daily	14
12	**Pentium 4 Computer Hard Disk Drive** operating 8 Hours Daily	19
13	**USB Flash Drive 128MB** Gift from Test Events of the Athens Olympics 2003 test events	20
14	**USB Flash Drive** I have with me every day	10
15	**USB Flash Drive** in non-daily use at home	15

As for how easily the USB Flash Drives burn out that I read on the Internet, I would like to point out that in the 16 years since 2003 when I got my first Flash Drive only two have been burnt and they were of poor quality)

All of the above, of course, on the one hand they were products from the most well-known and trusted companies and not on the cart with discounts from unknown sources and on the other hand, CD / DVD / BLU-RAY were not used on a daily basis, and kept in accordance with the manufacturer's instructions.

29. HARD COAT TECHNOLOGY

Hard Coat technology is based on the fact that on Blu-Ray, because the data layer is closer to the surface, scratches will make it easier unreadable. All companies have similar technologies to enhance scratch resistance with Verbatim's as the most well-known from which the term Hard Coat has generally prevailed.

Trying out an unbranded Blu-Ray disc with one featuring Hard Coat technology, after a total of 35 plays we see significantly less scratches or marks on the surface of the disc.

This automatically qualifies Hard Coat discs for archiving data and for backing up.

Not only Blu-Ray but also CDs and DVDs with Hard Coat technology are also marketed.

https://en.wikipedia.org/wiki/Blu-ray

30. M-DISC TECHNOLOGY

M-Disc technology named after the term Millenial Disc (from the company Milleniata which created it in 2009) with its inorganic coating (though more information is not known because of the secret patent) offers the greater resistance to optical storage than there is to date. The company claims that this record can stand up to 1000 years hence its name (at least theoretically).

https://en.wikipedia.org/wiki/M-DISC

Even the supreme US military service that has tested a disk with M-Disc technology in extreme conditions confirms its superiority.

https://web.archive.org/web/20130422110903if_/http://www.mdisc.com:80/docs/chinalakemillenniatatestreport_mod_04feb2010_a.pdf

The National metrology and testing laboratory (Laboratoire national de métrologie et d'essais) also concluded after tests that an M-Disc disc becomes unreadable after 500 hours of playback, while the average life of conventional discs does not exceed 250 hours.

https://www.lne.fr/sites/default/files/inline-files/duree-vie-DVDR-DVD-SYYLEX.pdf

Here again one could proceed with a theory similar to the one mentioned above, resulting in why not creating a disc that can withstand 1000, 2000 or 10,000 hours of playback.

The answer is simple. A specific technology disc is exclusively for those who want to archive important data at a high professional level (government records, military data, art collections, etc.) so in this case the disc will never be reproduced, (it will be stored in some special secure facility probably) unless perhaps other sources containing this data (and will certainly be many from hard drives, optical drives to cloud backups, etc.) have been destroyed.

Keeping it in perfect condition guarantees that no problem will ever occur.

And if we want a DVD or Blu-Ray disc to continuously play on a DVD player or one to watch favorite movies from it, we can make quite a few copies at minimal cost or even better to use a flash drive, without having to know anything about the M-Disc technology, because it's completely useless to such application.

31. LIGHTSCRIBE TECHNOLOGY

Lightscribe was an HP technology for labeling the surface of a CD / DVD with a specific coating, using the laser head of the recorder.

Released in 2004, HP stopped supporting product in 2013.

https://en.wikipedia.org/wiki/LightScribe

On the basis of digital archiving, many used Lightscribe discs for their digital archives, on the one hand for aesthetic reasons, and on the other to avoid writing on the disc with a marker, where according to some sources, was creating long-term damage the layers of the disc.

Using several Lightscribe discs, I did not see any difference in the durability with standard disc which there was writing with a marker on it, since of course a special marker labeled "CD Marker" was used.

There is only one case of a CD that has been recorded when someone tried to write to him with a rapidograph instead of a simple marker.

CDs and DVDs written with a marker, even simply indelible, and not marked "CD Marker" since 2001, have not had any reading problems. Of course, the recommended storage conditions (humidity-free environment, polypropylene pockets, etc.) are respected.

On Lightscribe CDs and DVDs also with an inscribed label, there is also no difference in durability but only an apparent fading, even though the label was inscribed with maximum contrast and storage conditions were met.

The study used CDs and DVDs only from well-known companies that hold the largest percent of the market.

Picture 64. Lightscribe CD audio disc from 2007, with apparent fading of the label (disregarding obvious iridescence during high resolution disc scanning)

32. HARD DRIVES (INTERNAL AND EXTERNAL, HDD - SSD), NAS, CLOUD

Here I will first mention the data storage process I use. I would like to stress de facto that I do not have state records to keep, but I have always been in favor of the security and reliability of the media.

Internal drives offer far greater security in data storage, as we do not, for example, have factors such as fall, which we often encounter in the external ones.

Let's also mention that with the growing capacities of SSD drives which are clearly more reliable than even the best conventional mechanical drive, Hard disk storage security, as for the internal drivers naturally, but also on external drives, is redefined.

The above is generally the consent of the technical community.

The main purpose of all of the projects I describe is the complete documentation of a multiple secure data storage system.

1. Files on the computer's hard disks (boot disk has Bitlocker encryption enabled)

2. File Backup to offline hard drives periodically, with encryption of important files.

3. Copy of the most important data to DVD / BLU-RAY and to a second set of hard drives in a different location.

I want to put a parenthesis here and say that any security protocol that respects itself should option for a second backup set of the data in a place other than the work / company or home.

4. Two NAS in the basement. The first you see below with two 4TB WD Red disks in RAID array for the most important data with no internet access and encryption. Provides instant Real Time Backup by synchronizing files and folders with my computer network. It also has a voltage stabilizer and UPS.

Note: I don't advertise products or sell any. I just use what I consider to be the most reliable and of course I have the financial ability to buy.

Picture 65. My Cloud Expert Series EX2 Ultra

https://www.wd.com/en-gb/products/network-attached-storage/my-cloud-expert-series-ex2-ultra.html

The second NAS is the one you see below, equipped with 4 4TB WD Red disks in RAID. It has two power supplies, a voltage stabilizer and a UPS, data encryption and direct synchronization of specific folders to a Cloud Backup provider.

This NAS also has an Internet connection, and through specially configured folders, it provides secure storage for files of relatives, friends, and coworkers that are instantly accessible, always encrypted, and synced to the Cloud.

Picture 66. My Cloud Expert Series EX4100

https://www.wd.com/products/network-attached-storage/my-cloud-ex4100.html

33. HUMAN PERSON CLOUD

By Human Person Cloud, I basically define a backup feature technique that involves acquaintances, friends, and relatives.

For orthopolitical reasons, I use for that manifested term the title "Human Person Cloud", since "Human Cloud" is already used in remote work applications, etc.

Under this term, scanning e.g., photos or other documents to files, and creating archives or digital albums of which we can give printed copies to relatives, if they referred to them, for example, along with a copy of the data on a DVD or a flash or an external disk. Provided, of course, that they are able to safeguard them.

Additionally, you can give an entire hard drive to a friend or relative ever with personal files for safekeeping without anyone else to know about it.

This will create an additional backup of your data, stored outside the home or the workplace.

Although studies have not been done theoretically it is as safe as a hard drive you have at home or cloud service, or perhaps a little less, at least as far as a human or a computer model can predict. Personally, I have created 17 examples of this technique and till now all are surviving.

You can always encrypt the particular removable drive you are about to give somewhere else (see section 20.1 for information).

34. FILE TRANSFERRING FROM OLD TYPE MOBILE PHONE, NON-SMART

With the fact that Smartphones have been in our lives for over 10 years now, it appears that young children of 18 years of age have never seen an old cell phone in their lives, except in the rare cases that they come across a device stored or seen mainly in the hands of senior citizens.

In this case, a Sony Ericsson K700i with a release date, March 2004, that is 15 years old, fell into my hands!

https://en.wikipedia.org/wiki/Sony_Ericsson_K700

https://www.gsmarena.com/sony_ericsson_k700-692.php

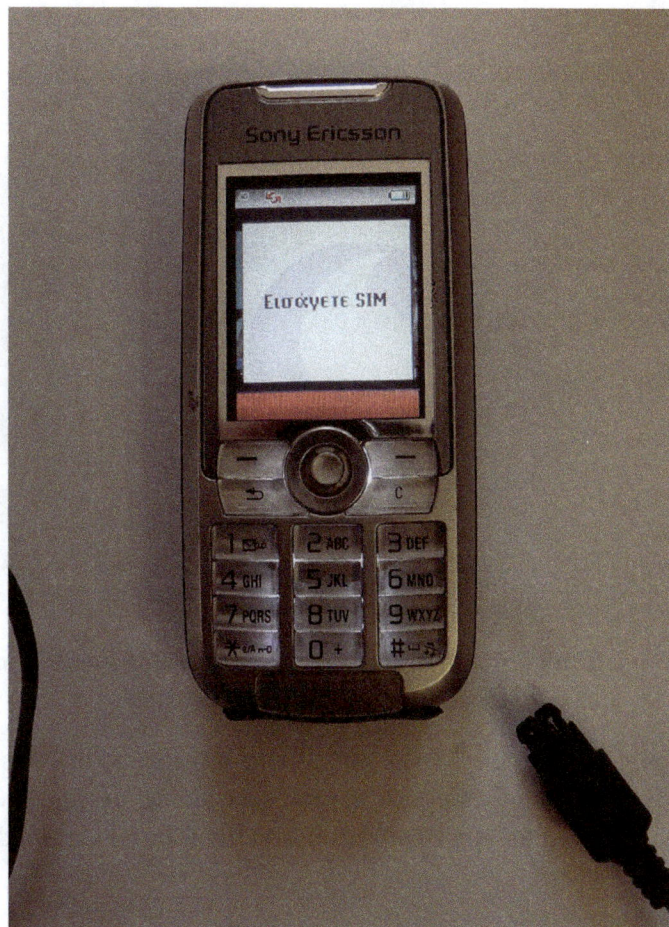

Picrure 67. Sony Ericsson K700i with its charger. The message that appears in screen in Greek language says "Enter SIM"

The task I was given was to retrieve photos from the device.

This is where the problems began.

I initially went to the stores of all the mobile carriers and the stereotypical answer I received was those adapters, cables and software they had for transferring files, contacts etc. are only for mobile Smartphones.

The only cable I had was the power supply. The USB Data Cable (DCU-11) was difficult to find even on ebay, and with cost of about 25 euros. There was also no guarantee that the device would be recognized in later versions of Windows except Windows XP and that it would generally work due to a malfunction even in a compatible operating system.

The cell phones of that era, unlike Smartphones, had no functions (applications, Internet browsing, etc.) without a SIM card.

For this very reason in the photo, you see the device displaying the "Insert SIM" message without allowing you to go through the menus and options.

There were two options: either I had to get a new standard sized SIM card, which was used by all the phones of that generation,

https://en.wikipedia.org/wiki/SIM_card

Or to use an adapter from Mini SIM to Micro or Nano SIM, of course I preferred the second way.

Pictures 68. From left to right: Micro SIM Adapter, Nano SIM Adapter an adjustable adapter between Micro και Nano SIM

Once the device was activated, I went to the menus and transferred the files with the only one option available to me, Bluetooth. High End Samsung and LG devices could not connect (apparently due to a different Bluetooth protocol), and the transfer was made with a 2014 Samsung Galaxy Core 2 device

https://www.gsmarena.com/samsung_galaxy_core_ii-6331.php

It took over 2 hours to transfer 40 files with total size of 37MB (photos and videos) due to the manual process and slow transfer speed.

Next goal was to transfer files from a 2009 Sony Ericsson W995

https://en.wikipedia.org/wiki/Sony_Ericsson_W995

70

Here things were definitely easier, though there was no data cable again.

I transferred all the data to the memory card and connected it to an adapter. The phone has a Memory Stick Micro (M2) for which the adapter is cheap and can be easily found both on eBay or other e-shops with a little searching.

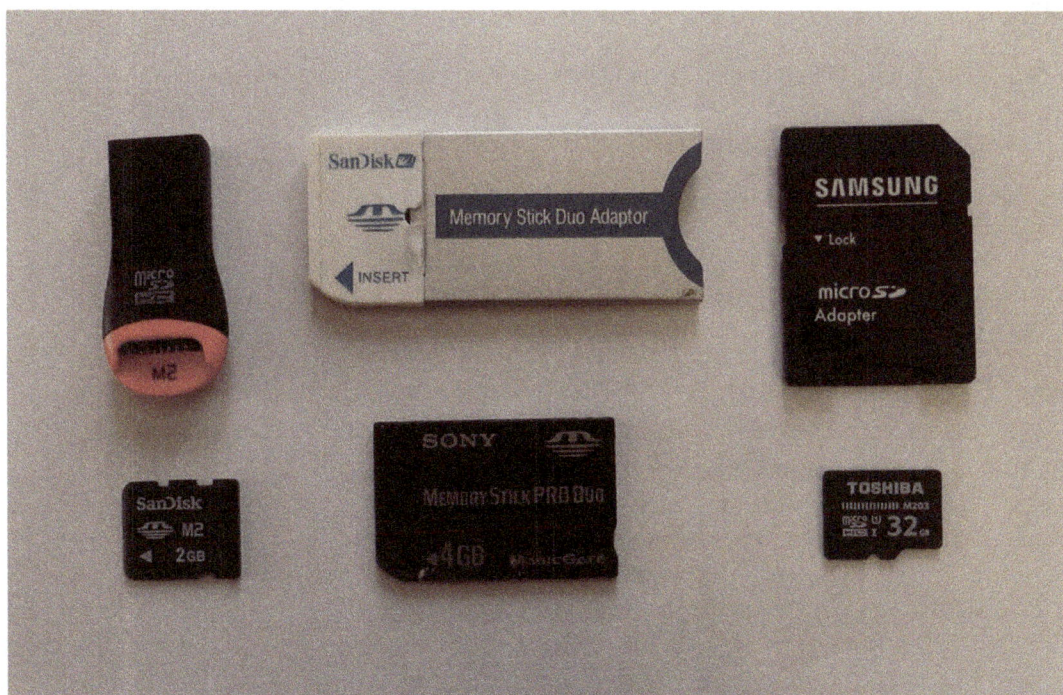

Picture 69. From left to right: Memory Stick Micro (M2) card (down) and an adapter to USB (up), Memory Stick PRO Duo card (down) and adapter (up) and finally a contemporary Micro SD card which is utilized by the majority of the Smartphones at this moment (down) and an adapter to SD card (This is the type of card usually available on photo cameras and many laptops also have a slot for such cards (up)

35. TRANSFER OF A VIDEO CD (VCD) TO FILE

The Video CD appeared in 1993 and remained on the market until at least 2000 in Greece where before the crisis every weekend or even daily, all newspapers VCD as a gift.

When the cost of systematic DVD production dropped, the VCD disappeared.

https://en.wikipedia.org/wiki/Video_CD

Moving the contents of a VCD to a mpeg or avi file is essential for many reasons.

In our times, Hard Drives and USB Flash Drives have huge capacities, so it's easier and more straightforward to play a video file from them, rather than searching for the disc and inserting it into a CD/DVD Player.

The disc may well have worn out or may no longer be readable due to aging since it is theoretically 15 to 25 years old.

Moving the VCDs to a file also reduces the space occupied by them since we can then send them for recycling or burn to a 25 GB Blu-ray Disc (actual 23 GB capacity) from 30 to 35 VCDs.

If it was a movie, I don't think it's worth the effort, since you can find it on DVD, Blu-Ray or even watch it online since we're in the age of streaming.

In this particular case I owned a series of documentaries that the television no longer airs and it was generally difficult to find them elsewhere.

The process is relatively simple and does not take much time for each disk since they do not have large data size due to the low resolution.

I used The Ultimate VCD Ripper by Elite Minds Inc (Shareware) from cnet.com

https://download.cnet.com/Ultimate-VCD-Ripper/3000-2194_4-75279796.html

The file created has an average size of 500 to 700MB with the standard VCD resolution of 352x388 pixels.

The project was completed smoothly, however I decided to digitize both the covers and the VCD itself.

I could do the process again with the EPSON V370 scanner which would take a long time even at low resolutions which makes a quick scan since you have to put in and put out disks and covers from the scanner glass, so I thought of another way.

Picture 70. Wine gift case for two bottles which was used as a stand for taking photos of the covers and the VCD

Picture 71. Adjusting a Samsung Galaxy A3 with 14MP camera. In this way there was a perfect stability while taking the shots. In the wine case holes we could fit even a compact digital camera.

At the bottom, in a good distance from the camera I placed the VCD and the covers and adjusted slightly the zoom in.

The result was perfect with sharp copies in high resolution all concentrated in the memory of the mobile phone and easily transferred to the computer.

I found the wine case quite easily in a liquor store. Although you can devise other ways to do the same work. I gave the idea, Try it out!

The same procedure for transferring a DVD or Blu-Ray in a file could be done by using an equivalent rip program like

http://www.xilisoft.com/dvd-ripper.html or http://www.xilisoft.com/blu-ray-ripper.html

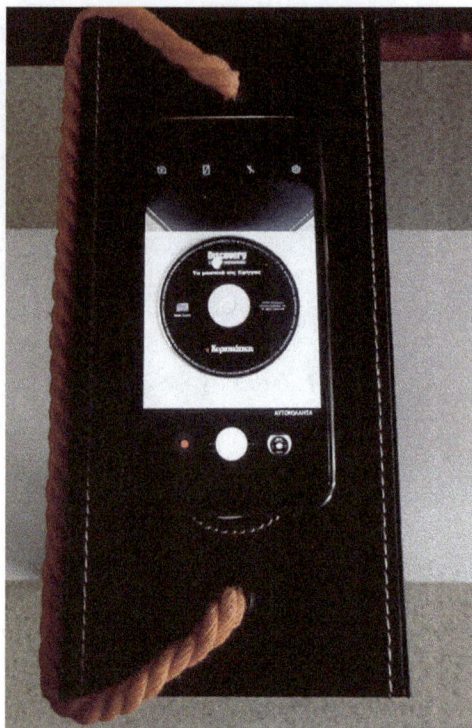

Picture 72. The result of a photo shot from above

36. VHS CASSETTE DIGITIZATION

Many of us still have home VHS cassettes at home with family moments, trips, conferences, etc.

Although the video has existed since the 1970s, in Greece it enjoyed moments of glory in the 1980s with well-known Greek video movie productions, until the emergence of private television in Greece in the early 1990s.

https://en.wikipedia.org/wiki/Videocassette_recorder

Although video devices were manufactured until 2016, mainly in DVD / VCR format (a combination of both devices) and cassettes are still available for sale even in large supermarkets, (not only for standard VHS but also for camcorders) almost no one has a video at home anymore.

https://en.wikipedia.org/wiki/VCR/DVD_combo

After the completion of the digital transition (on 2012 in Athens, Attica, Greece) to DVB-T Mpeg4, since the video could only record an analogue signal, VHS videos became useless since it had to be connected with an external Mpeg4 decoder to have signal and this could only work on certain models and compatibility conditions.

https://el.wikipedia.org/wiki/Digea

There was a need for a doctor to digitize all the surgical operations he had made in his career that he had videotaped.

I have purchased in 2008 an LG V-190 VCR/DVD Combo

https://www.amazon.co.uk/LG-V-190-DVD-VHS-Combo/dp/B00186J85S

Manual in English:

https://gscs-b2c.lge.com/downloadFile?fileId=KROWM000185630.pdf

LG later released some more advanced models with HDMI output and the ability to record directly from a Videotape to DVD, options that the V192 didn't have, so I had to work with the RCA outputs.

Picture 73. LG V192 VHS Video -DVD

The triple RCA output you see in the bottom right corresponds to: yellow for the video and white and red for the two audio channels

https://en.wikipedia.org/wiki/RCA_connector

By ending up with this solution, now I had to connect it with my PC, through the internal TV Tuner I have, AverMedia, model H777 Hybrid DVB-T

https://web.archive.org/web/20150329184837/https://www.nextworld.in/product.aspx?sku=HW8749

There are also compact devices that perform the same process, but without good quality and with problematic or zero support for Windows 8, Windows 10, Windows 11 etc. operating systems.

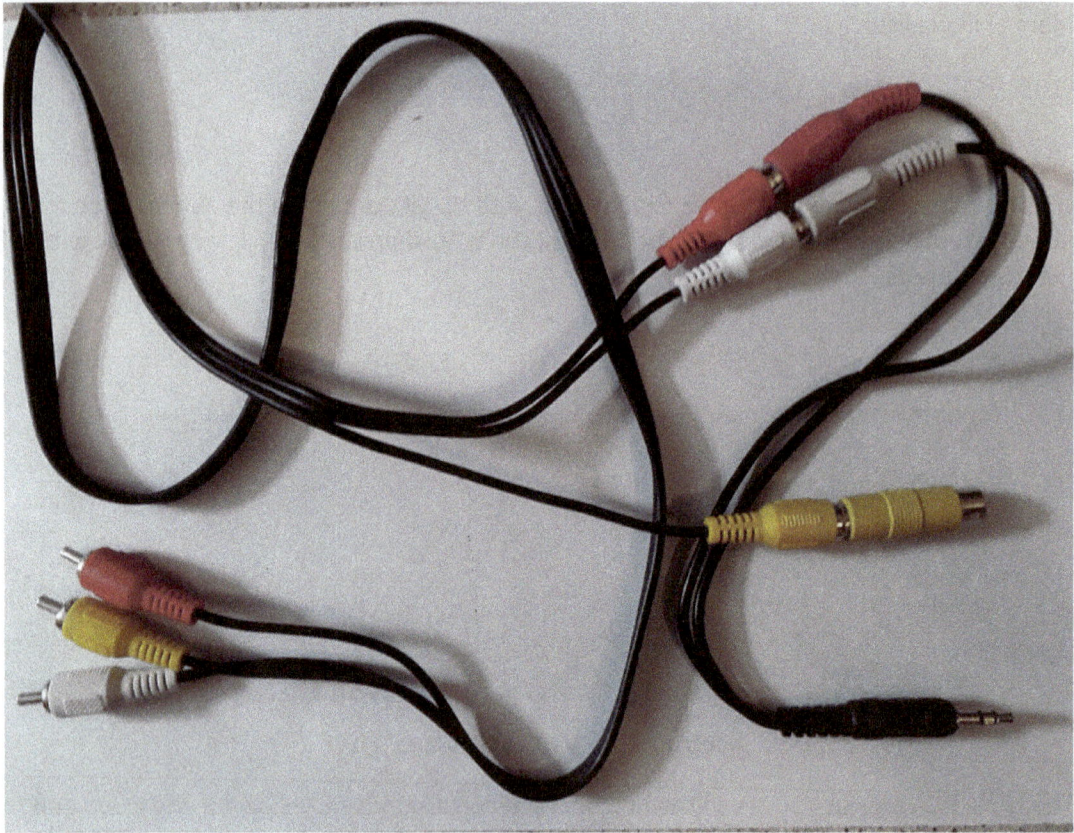

Picture 74. RCA to S-Video cable

The wiring is as follows: The three RCAs seen above in the video, end up the video (yellow) to the adapter for SVideo and white and red (the two audio channels) to a 3.5 jack

For SVideo see here

https://en.wikipedia.org/wiki/S-Video

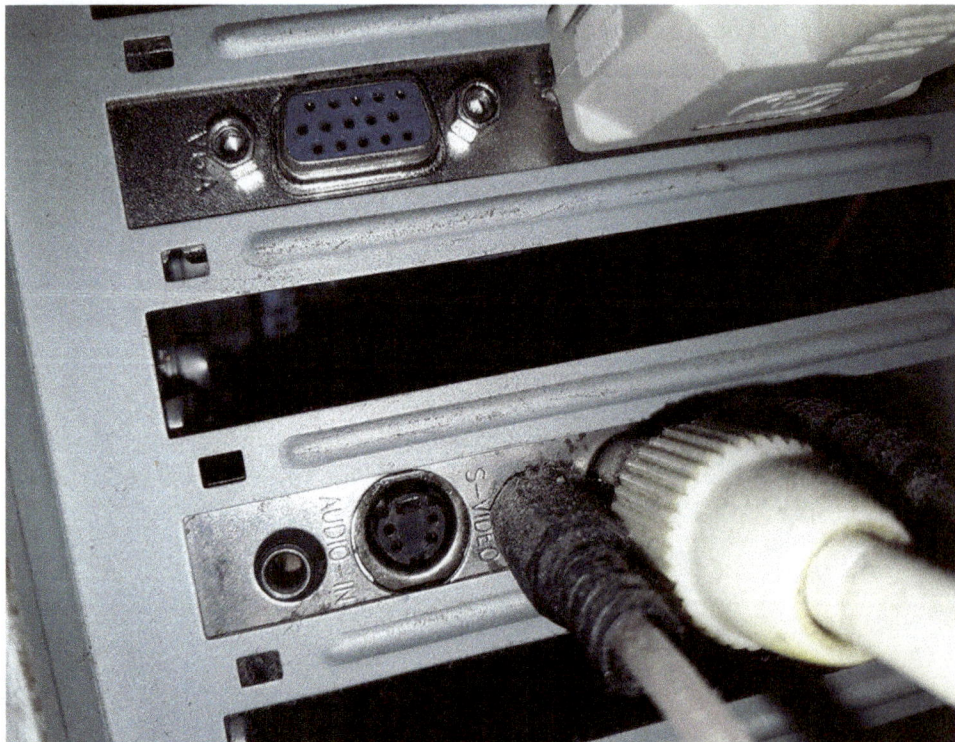

Picture 75. SVideo connection

The back of the computer tower with the ports of the AverMedia TV Tuner visible. The yellow cable with the SVideo adapter connects to the corresponding port (similar to PS/2), while the white and red (the two audio channels) to the Audio In connector through the 3.5 jack.

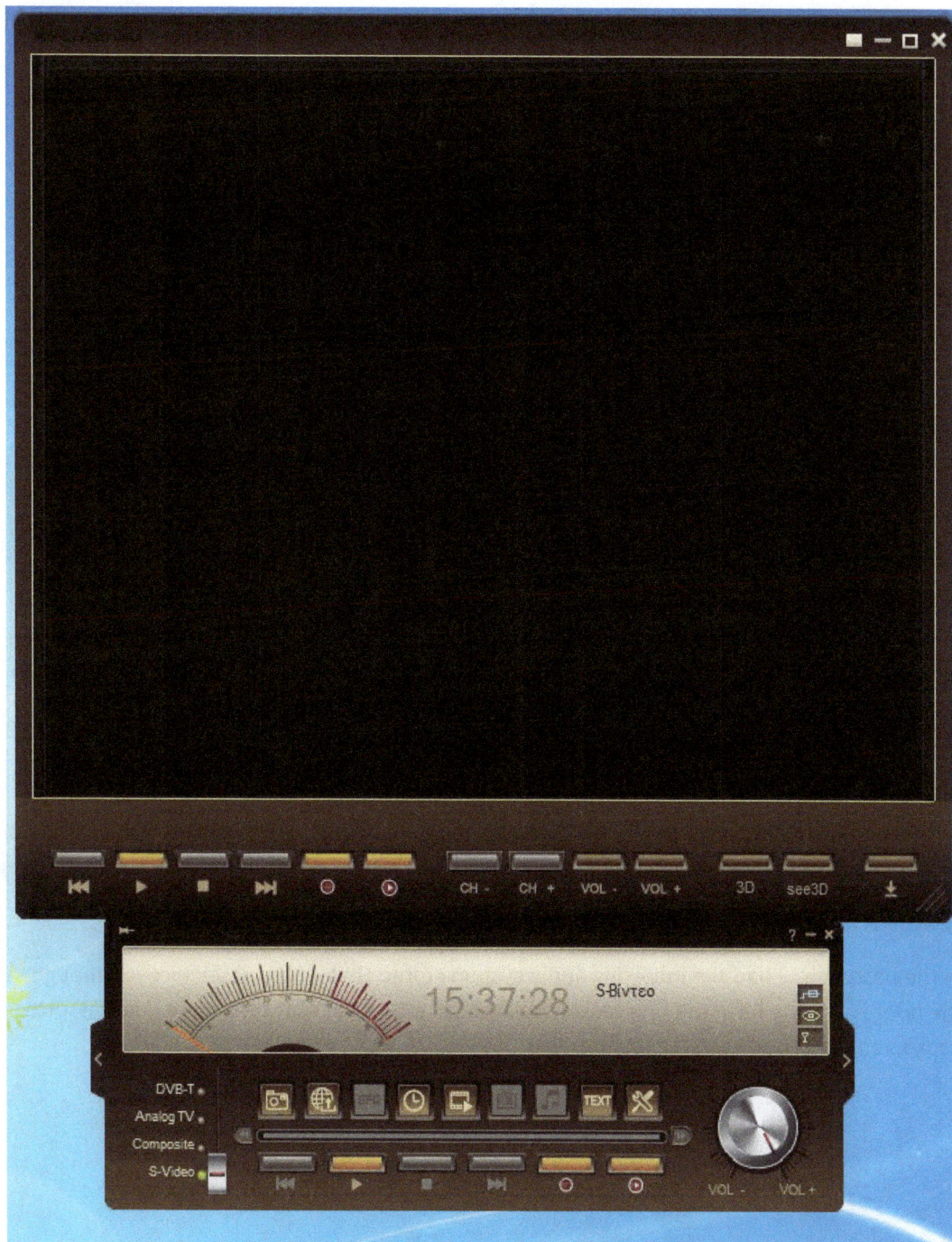

Picture 76. AverMedia TV 3D Application

The next step is to start the AverMedia TV 3D application and set the input to the SVideo option by tapping Play from the video and recording from the application to begin digitizing.

The setting for the output file was 720x576 (DVD-like) and Bitrate 5000. This gives a very good result even on Full HD screens.

The image quality has to do with many parameters of course, such as the quality of the original recording source, e.g., analogue television with poor signal, old video camera and the age and condition of the cassette.

Indicative digitized file sizes:

Duration	Size
1 hour, 14 minutes	2.78 GB
44 minutes	1.65 GB
55 minutes	2.07 GB
1 hour, 22 minutes	3.07 GB

37. AUDIO TAPE DIGITIZATION

The audio cassettes also had their heyday in Greece at least, from 1970 to 1990, taking the lead from vinyl records and in turn were replaced by CDs.

https://en.wikipedia.org/wiki/Cassette_tape

As weird as it may seem, audio tapes and cassette players can still be found in Greece (though in limited numbers) and many have a cassete Hi-Fi system at home that works even though we used it only as a radio. I have also seen many reporter audio cassette recorders in use. (Weird enough since there are digital models with an SD card for a decade or more now and most reporters, they just use their mobile phone to do their work.)

Where do all these cassettes still come from and why they don't get a digital memory model or their cellphone for recording is a wonder, although in Greece you can many old technologies still in use.

So here is also the need to digitize the contents of an audio cassette into an mp3 file.

In the basement, I had the following audio system stored that works perfectly even though the door is missing from the one cassette player (all models of that time were dual cassette deck to copy the one cassette to another)

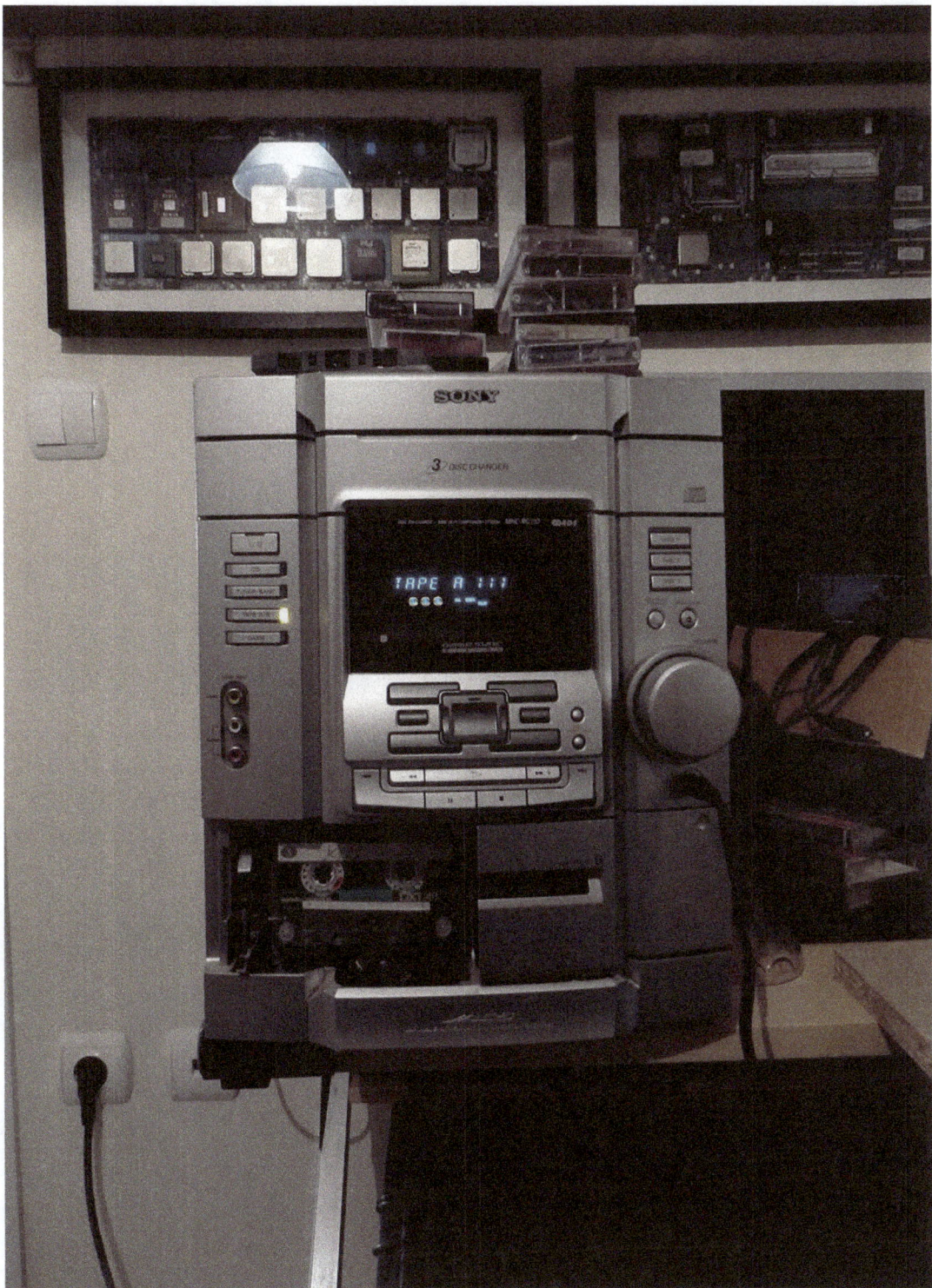

Picture 77. The Sony dual deck cassette Hi-Fi system is the one you see below which even had the ability to mount three CDs. The process is very simple. We connect a 3.5 jack cable to the headphone output and the other side of the cable connects in the Line In port at the computer's sound card.

Picture 78. Of course, we don't get into trouble of digitizing old commercial tapes when the entire repertoire is on Youtube (even though illegally), but tapes with songs from the band we had create when we were teenagers or the ones, I found below with Takis Fotiou's recordings (or tfot from the nickname he used on the Internet) from Jeronimo Groovy (old Radio Station in Athens, Greece)

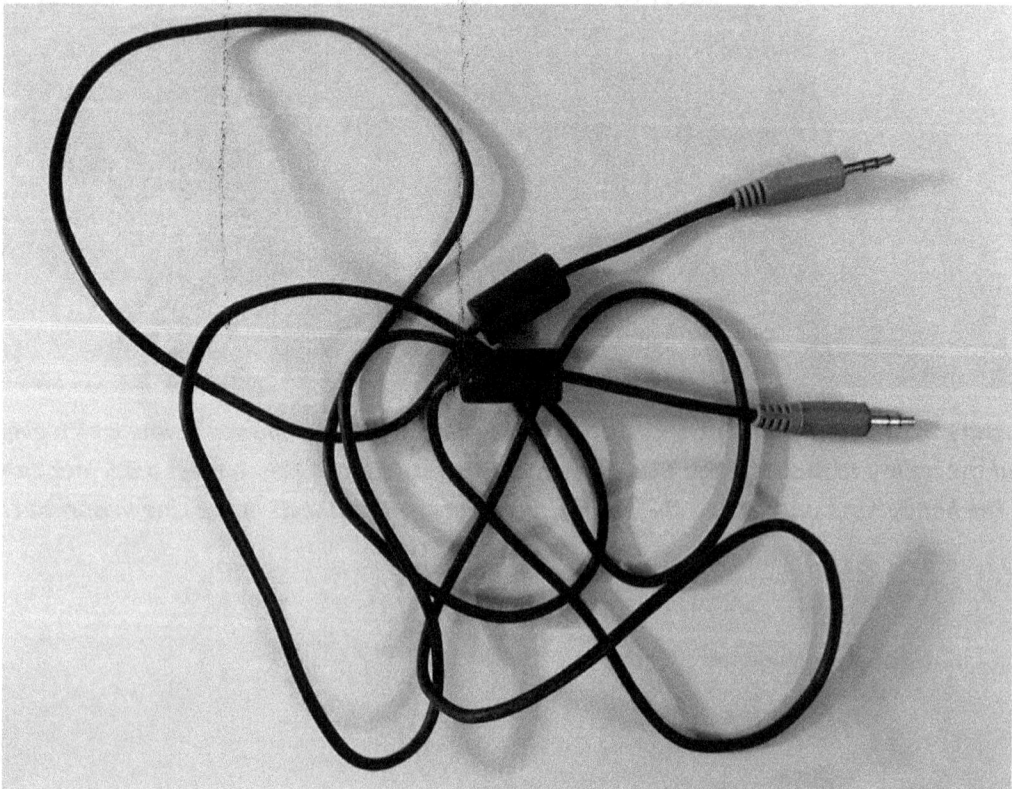

Picture 79. 3.5 to 3.5 jack cable

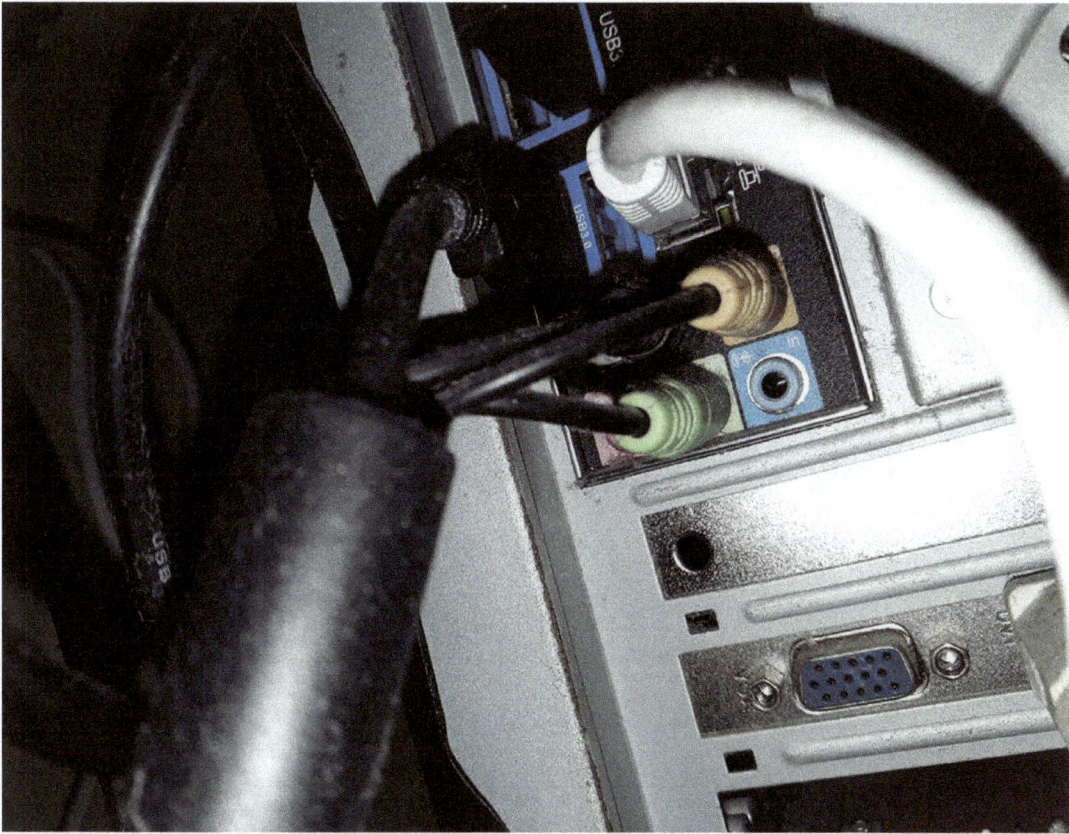

Picture 80. Audio in port on the back side of the computer

This model incorporated a very good equalizer system very useful for treble and bass corrections as well to reduce the cassette background sound noise

The rest of the work is done by Audacity, a free Windows audio recorder.

https://www.audacityteam.org/

Just press Play on the cassette player and simultaneously record on the Audacity. The only problem, as with video cassettes, is that you have to wait for the cassette to finish playing until you can stop recording and save the file.

I first saved the file in wav (compression-free format for maximum quality) and then made an mp3 file at 320kbps (maximum quality) excessive quality someone would say but now with the capacity available on hard disks, a 40MB audio file is not a luxury for few.

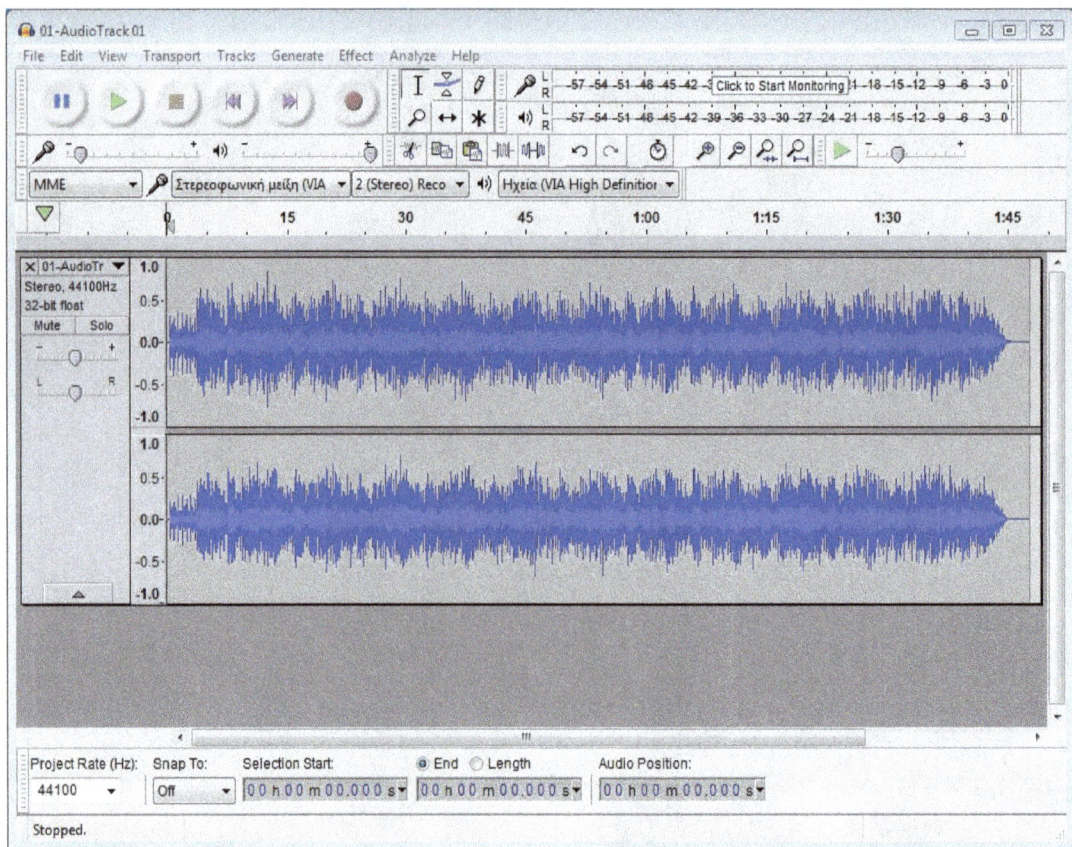

Εικόνα 81. The Audacity is probably the best and most reliable free sound recorder program on Windows

38. MAGNETIC TAPE DIGITIZATION

What you will see below is a reel-to-reel tape recorder.

https://www.radiomuseum.org/r/grundig_tk20.html

To Grundig TK20 was first produced in 1958, has tubes instead of transistors and operates with a 7.5 inch magnetic tape.

https://en.wikipedia.org/wiki/Magnetic_tape

for the tubes (predecessors of transistors see below)

https://en.wikipedia.org/wiki/Vacuum_tube

There is still today a huge debate on the internet if the tubes produce better quality sound that the transistors.

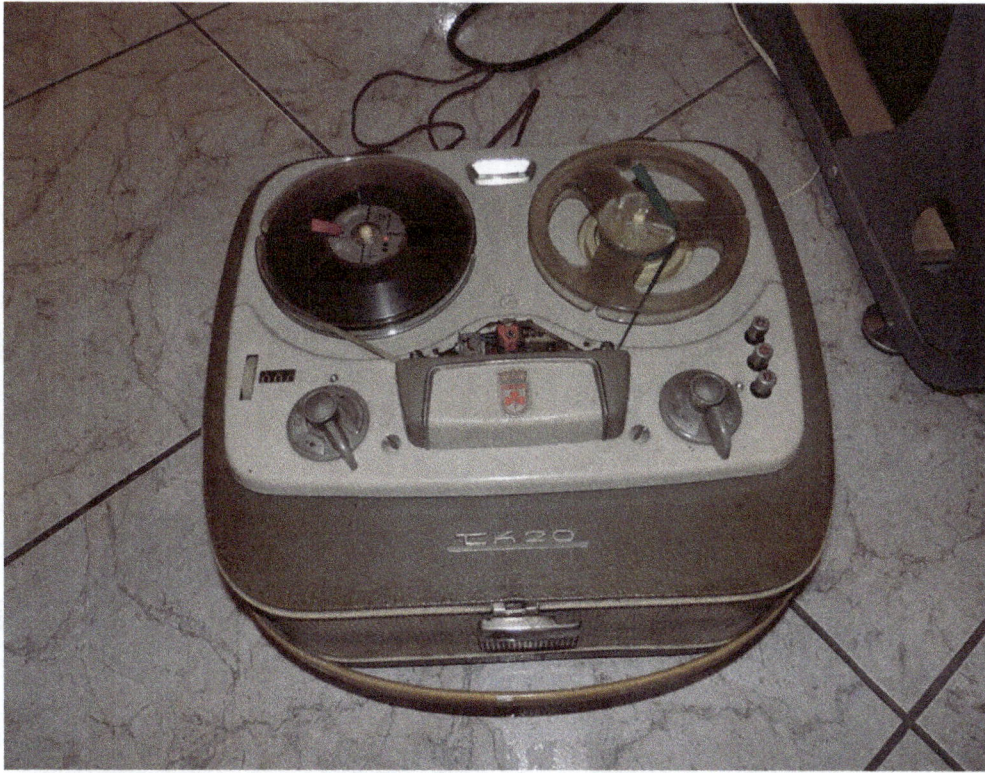

Picture 82. Back to our project. I had in my hand a fully operational machine and one magnetic tape. My goal like in all the other projects was the digitization of the tape.

The device had in back side, outlets with plugs you could not find in the market, let alone cable, and each outlet had various "hieroglyphs" on it that only the manufacturer knew what it had in mind.

Picture 83. Finding the manual on the internet, "decrypted" the symbols and tried to put in cables to output audio, but rust and antiquity had made the slots useless.

Noticing that the value of the device did not exceed 60-70 euros on eBay in many cases, I decided to go for a more invasive method, if you are a vintage lover and cannot bear the sight, do not read below.

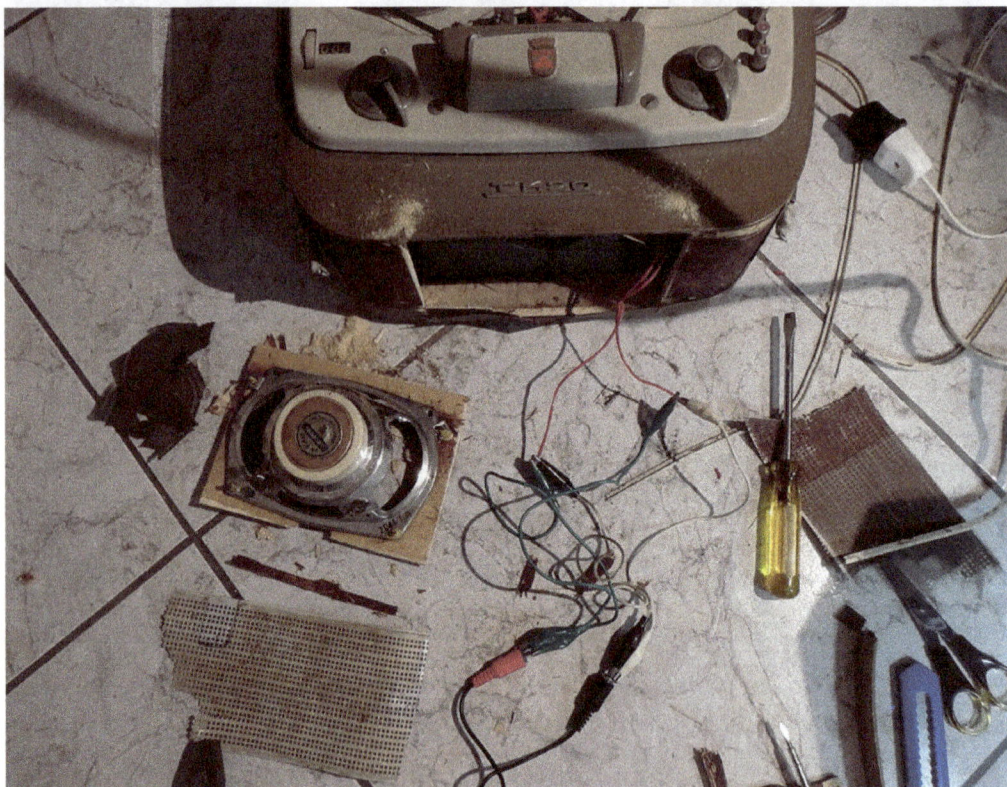

Picture 84. I sawed the front of the tape recorder, and at the outputs of the loudspeaker with crocodile connectors I connected a cable with RCA plugs.

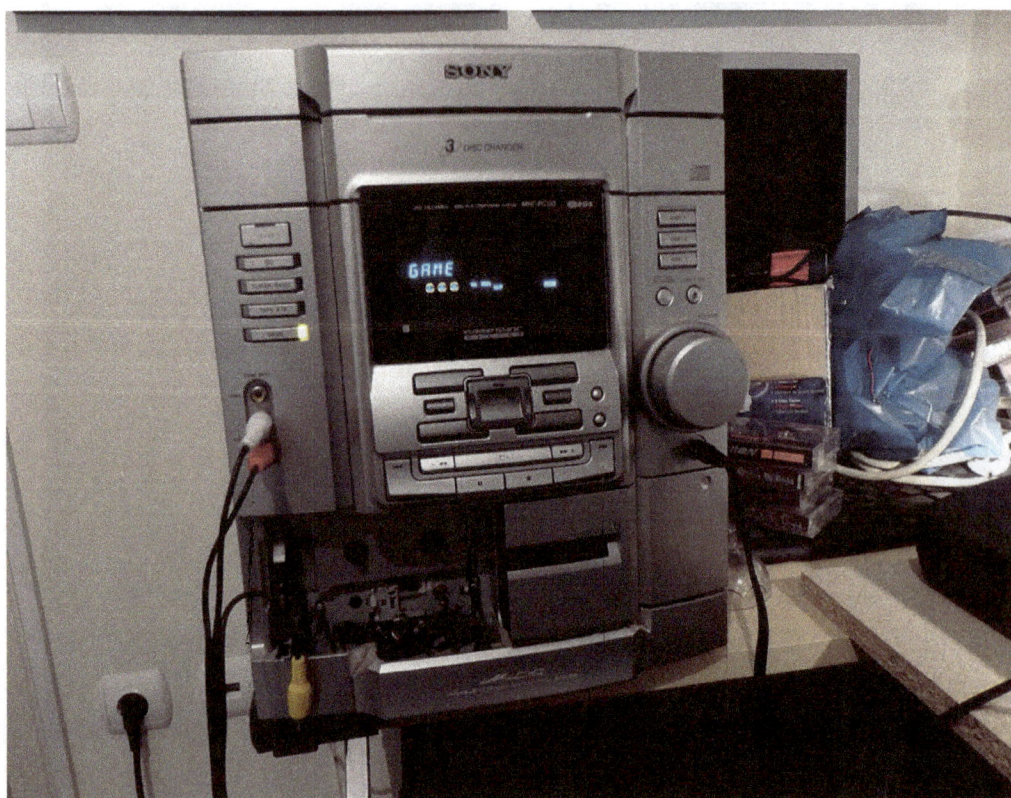

Picture 85. Connection of the tape recorder to the Hi-Fi audio system and sending the audio to the computer via a 3,5 jack to the Line In port.

After researching the Internet, there have been many reports that connecting an old record player, or similar device equipped with tubes (pre-transistor era), due to the audio high output voltage or watts, often the audio chipset of the computer burned. Some have suggested a USB sound card as a solution which again I don't think that eliminates the risk of damage. So, I preferred to plug the RCA plugs into the HI-FI audio system (taking advantage of the digital equalizer) and then plug the 3.5 jack into the headphone jack of the Hi-Fi and then into the Audio In the computer.

Note that the device is of course monophonic not stereo. But I bridged the audio channels on both RCA plugs to create two channels recording rather than mono.

The process from then on continued without further excitement. With Audacity, as in the previous cases I made two recordings (one with treble and one with bass profile) in uncompressed wav format and then converted them to 320kbps mp3.

The Grundig then was led to recycling, which should be the rule for electronic devices, not the exception.

39. VINYL RECORD DIGITIZATION

I also own a 1966 Perpetuum-Ebner PE66 turntable, remanufactured. It was originally housed in furniture as was the fashion of those days for built-in pickup furniture, buffet with lighting and later a radio. I transferred it and with the help of a carpenter I adapted it to a wooden construction. This also works with tubes.

https://www.radiomuseum.org/r/perpetuum_plattenwechsler_pe66_pe_6.html

Picture 86. Here is the Perpetuum-Ebner PE66 in the special wooden construction, fully operational.

I have used the same method here as above, with the tape recorder for digitizing a record just for demonstration. Although the turntable is monophonic several records were in stereo mode but forced to mono.

There was no reason to digitize an entire record collection with the above device as vinyl is doing a comeback and has become a trend mainly in the younger ages, so there are modern turntables on the market even from many branded manufacturers, with audio enhancement technologies and a built-in USB port, to digitize the record directly during playback.

Below are some models for reference.

https://www.whathifi.com/sony/ps-hx500/review

https://www.amazon.co.uk/Akai-ATT01U-ATT-01U-Turntable/dp/B001KXAERU

https://shopping.mercatos.com/en/thomson-encoder-turntable-black-_pid4601021.html#

40. FILE TRANSFERING FROM 3.5 AND 5.25 FLOPPY DISKS

We left the floppy disks almost last for historical reasons. Transferring files from a 3.5-inch floppy disk is a very easy process, once that is available on both eBay and many other sites, a 3.5-inch floppy disk to USB drive. There is also an all-in-one driver on the market along with a usb card reader that can be connected internally to a computer tower. The devices are compatible with any version of Windows.

Picture 87. 3.5-inch Floppy Disk Drive to σε USB

For 5.25-inch disks, things are infinitely more difficult. They had already retired several years before the 3.5, and of course 5.25 floppy disk drive was never produced on USB adapter. Searching the internet there are some solutions for an amateur USB connection, but with many limitations.

http://www.deviceside.com/fc5025.html

I had a 5.25-inch driver so the problem was where to plug it in to read the disks.

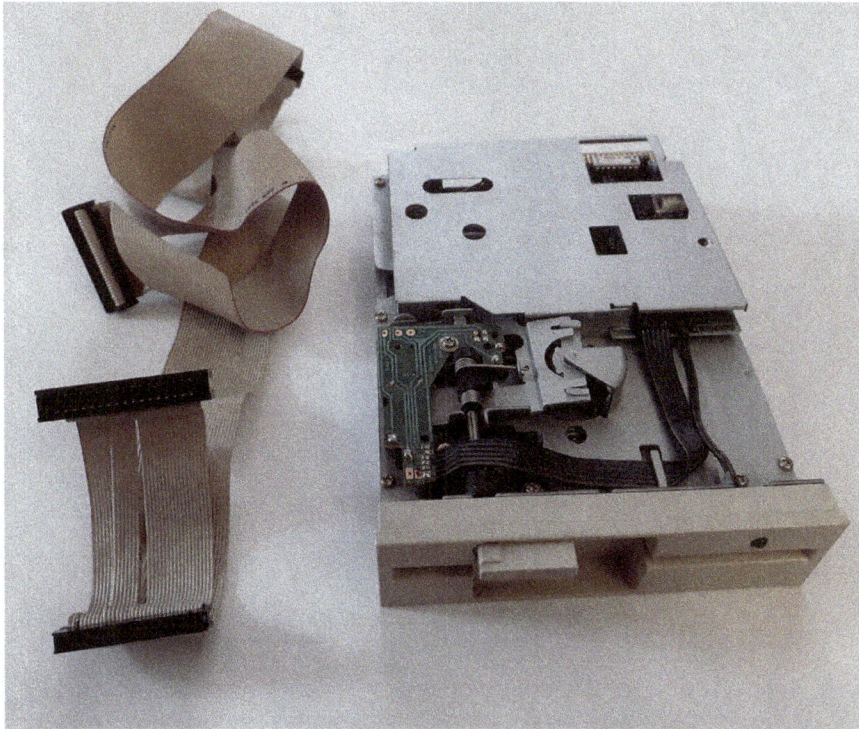

Picture 88. 5.25-inch floppy disk drive and a tape cable. (The 3.5 drive had a different interface than the 5.25 so the tape cable had also two interfaces for each type, e.g., to connect two 3.5 drives or two 5.25s)

In this case, I recruited a Windows 98 Pentium III capable of connecting 2 floppy drives (Usually defined as 3.5 inches (Drive A) and 5.25 inches (Drive B). That is why the hard drive still gets the letter C from the system even in 2019 computers, since A and B are firmly reserved for floppy drives even though they haven't been installed anymore on computers for many years now)

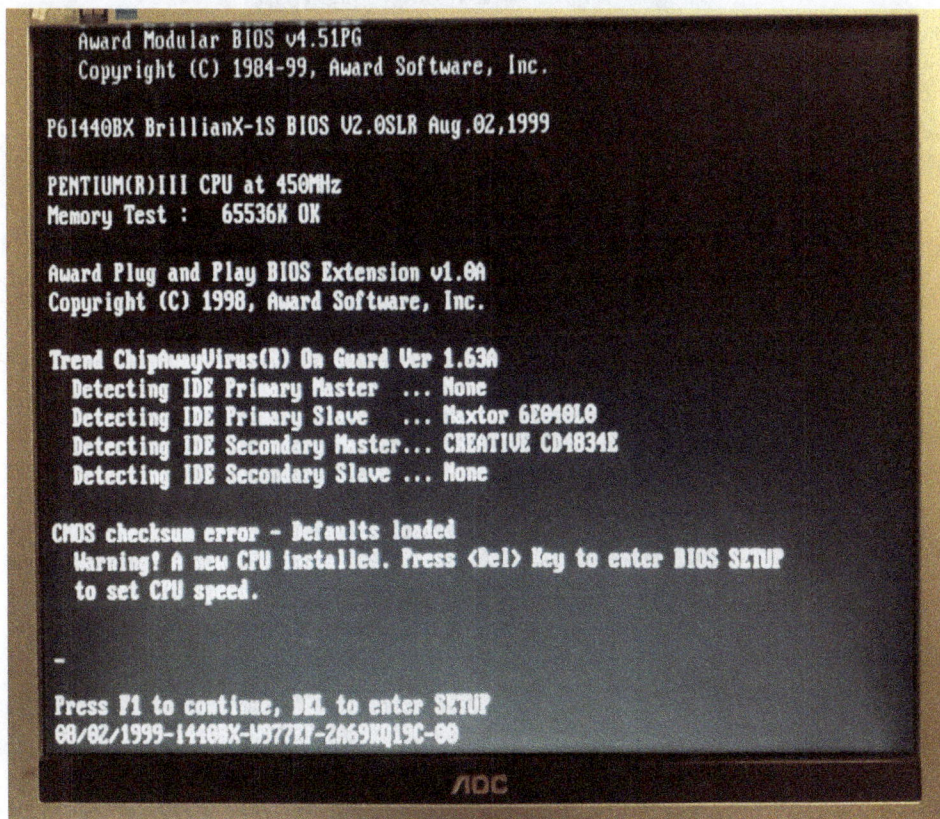

Picture 89. Pentium III BIOS posting

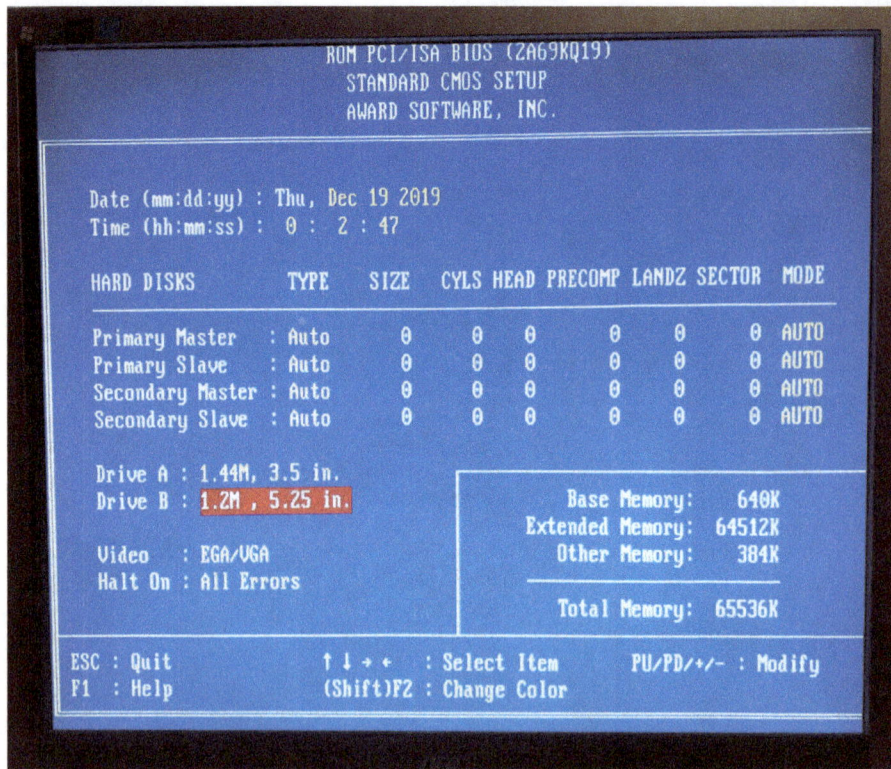

```
              ROM PCI/ISA BIOS (ZA69KQ19)
                 STANDARD CMOS SETUP
                 AWARD SOFTWARE, INC.


   Date (mm:dd:yy) : Thu, Dec 19 2019
   Time (hh:mm:ss) :  0 :  2 : 47

   HARD DISKS        TYPE   SIZE  CYLS HEAD PRECOMP LANDZ SECTOR  MODE

   Primary Master   : Auto    0     0    0      0     0      0   AUTO
   Primary Slave    : Auto    0     0    0      0     0      0   AUTO
   Secondary Master : Auto    0     0    0      0     0      0   AUTO
   Secondary Slave  : Auto    0     0    0      0     0      0   AUTO

   Drive A : 1.44M, 3.5 in.
   Drive B : 1.2M , 5.25 in.           ┌─────────────────────────────┐
                                       │   Base Memory:      640K    │
   Video  : EGA/VGA                    │ Extended Memory:  64512K    │
   Halt On : All Errors                │    Other Memory:    384K    │
                                       │                             │
                                       │   Total Memory:   65536K    │
                                       └─────────────────────────────┘

   ESC : Quit              ↑ ↓ → ←  : Select Item    PU/PD/+/- : Modify
   F1  : Help             (Shift)F2 : Change Color
```

Picture 90. Pentium III - Setting a 5.25-inch drive in the BIOS manually.

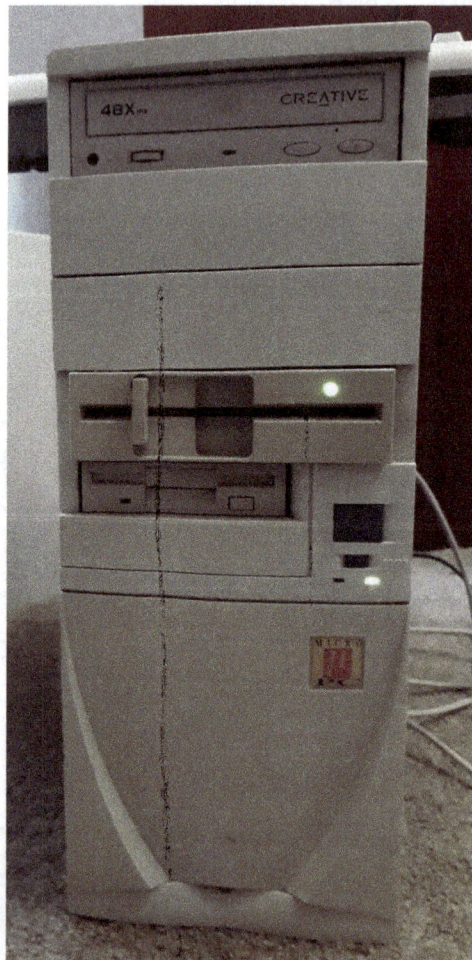

Picture 91. Pentium III tower with a 3.5 and 5.25-inch drives. The is a disk inserted in the 5.25 drive

So, after we connected the drive to the computer and set it manually in the BIOS (old computers couldn't automatically see most devices, (like old users would remember you had to manually enter even the size of the hard drive, heads and cylinders) we installed a 5.25-inch floppy disk that the computer can read without problems.

Here are 4 pictures from the Windows 98 environment

Picture 92. (left) Windows 98 Desktop.

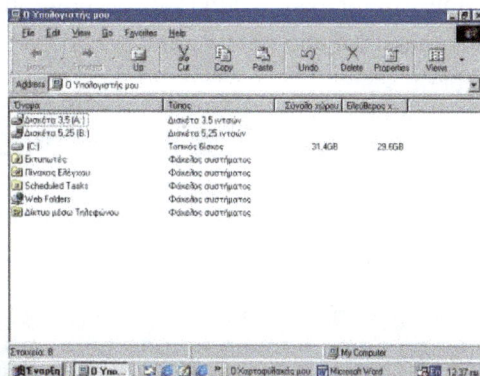

Picture 93. (right) the Windows 98 "My Computer" window open των where we can see the floppy drives and the hard drive.

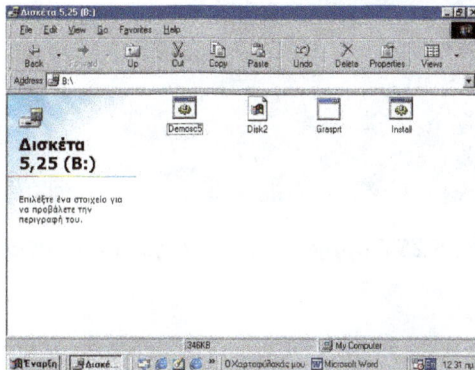

Picture 94. (left) Explorer window with the contents of a 5.25 inch floppy disk of 1991. Allthough that 28 years have passed the files where intact.

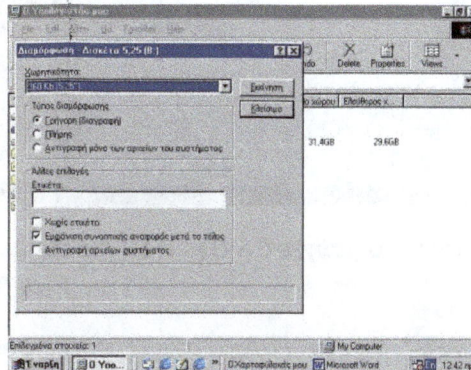

Picture 95. (right) format of a 5.25 floppy disk of 360KB capacity.

I would like to emphasize that as I mentioned at the beginning that the demonstration with the Pentium III was made to show that even a computer 20 years of the 1999 can boot without much effort and even perform tasks such as copying files, accessing the Internet (although in Internet Explorer 4 no modern webpage will open properly) as well as word processing.

This proves that data that we often consider permanently lost due to the age of the storage media or the computer is not and can be recovered.

The whole process, as long as we have the 5.25 drive and the tape cable to connect it, can also be done on a motherboard e.g., *Gigabyte GA-G33M-S2* of 2007 which supports Core 2 Duo and Core 2 Quad processors and was one of the last to have a Floppy Disk Drive and IDE Hard Drive controller. In practice with this motherboard, we can read 5.25 disks even under a Windows 10 (or even a Windows 11) environment. (In this case of course we can only connect one drive and not two as it was possible on old computers but this problem is negligible).

https://www.gigabyte.com/Motherboard/GA-G33M-S2-rev-1x

Naturally we did this too.

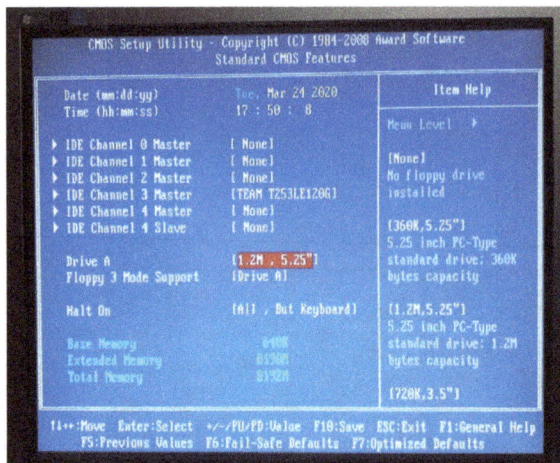

Picture 96. Gigabyte GA-G33M-S2 Motherboard, 5.25 Floppy Drive Settings in the BIOS (left).

Picture 97. Gigabyte GA-G33M-S2 Motherboard with 34 pins Floppy connector on down right corner - (right).

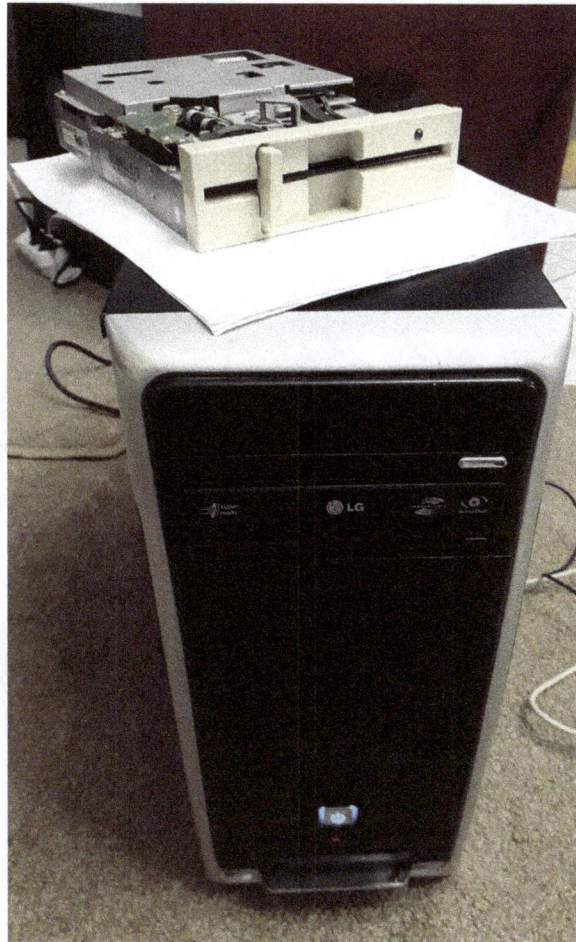

Picture 98. Core 2 Quad Q6600 CPU Tower PC with a 5.25-inch floppy drive.

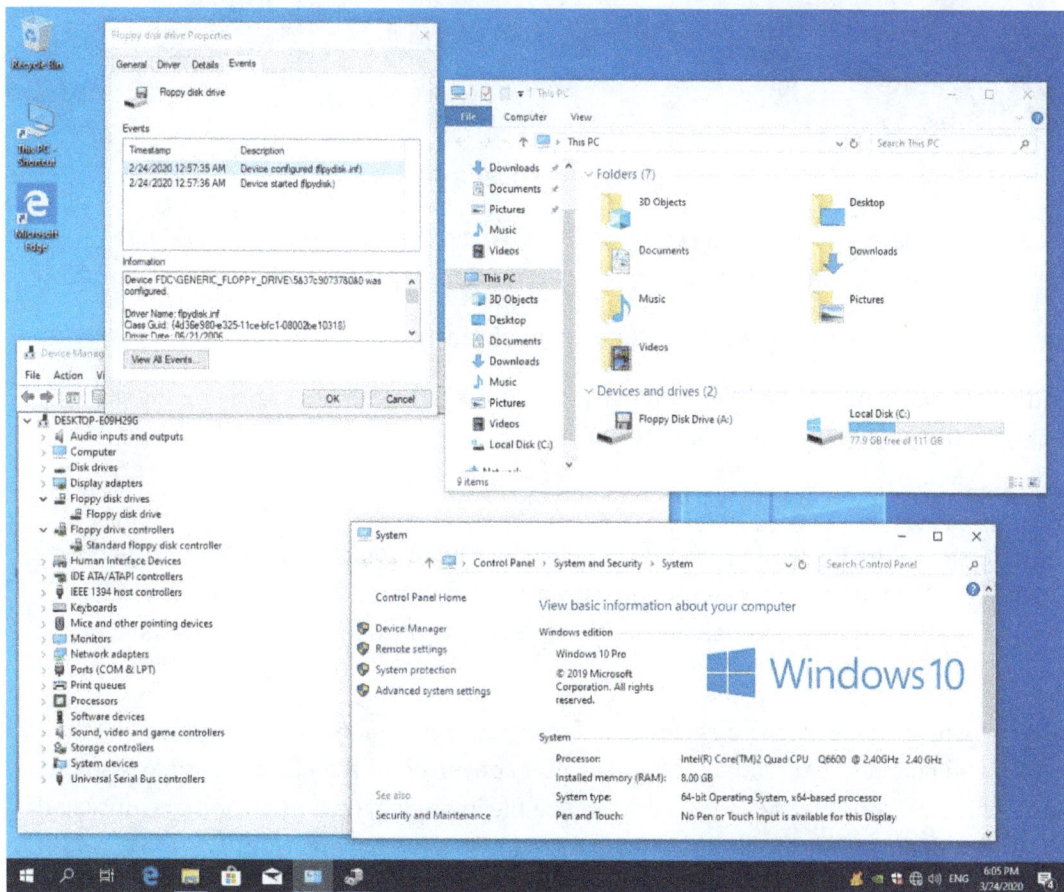

Picture 99. 5.25 Floppy Drive Install on Windows 10.

41. SUPER 8 FILM DIGITIZATION

The Super 8 mm film was a motion-picture film format released in 1965 by Kodak. Corporation

For more information refer to the correspondent Wikipedia article:

https://en.wikipedia.org/wiki/Super_8_film

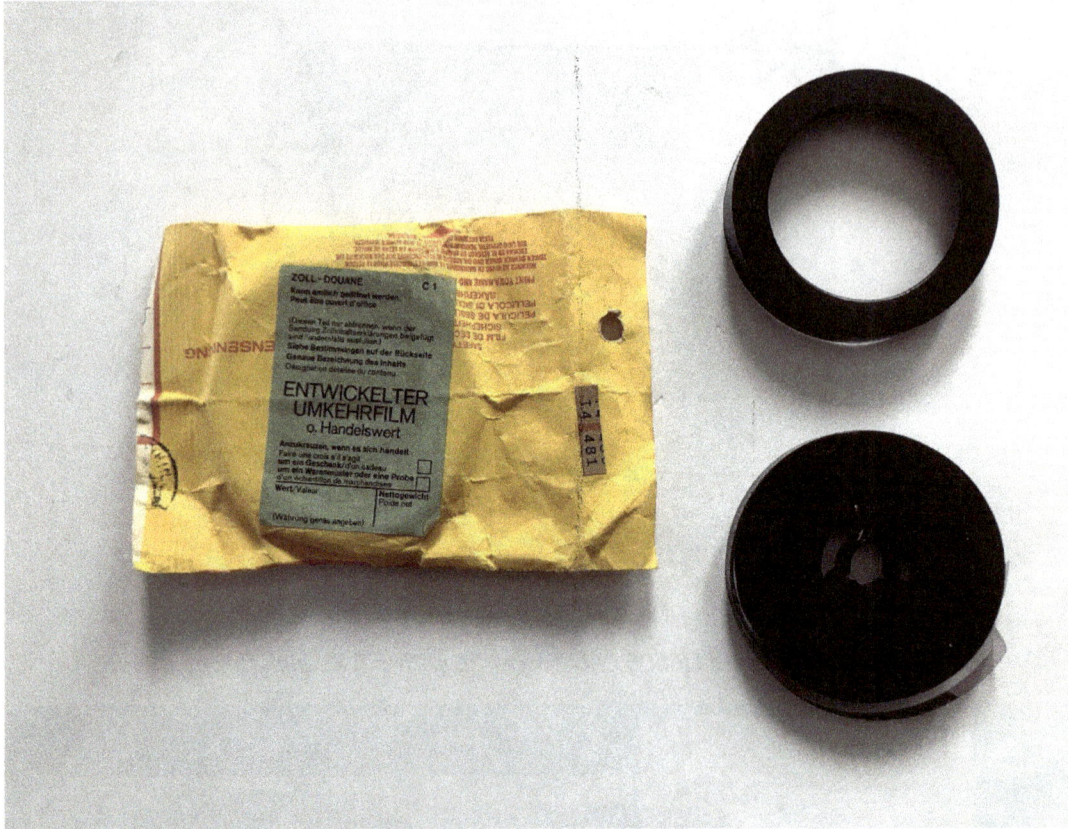

Picture 100. Super 8 Film

Since I didn't have a Super 8 projection machine, I gave the only one film I had (with duration 3 minutes and 20 seconds) to two different photography shops for digitization.

Prior to the conversion I asked about the quality of the exported file.

Both shops had dedicated conversion machines, while a third one was playing the film and recorded the projection with a digital camera.

They told me that the quality will be as "good as possible".

In the first one the file was an .avi file with size 497MB and video resolution upscaled to 1920x1080 (the film is of course with an aspect ratio of 4:3 and left and right were black fillings) and the other a dvd quality .vob file of 158MB and video resolution 720x576 of unacceptable quality.

Be careful in advance when you give a film for digitization and ask to be informed specifically for the equipment they use and that you want it converted to the higher possible resolution (for archival reasons ideally you can ask for one file in original resolution and one upscaled, not with a video editing program but from the conversion machine itself)

In various e-shops with keywords "8mm film digital converter" you can find a lot of products available, but I'm afraid I can't tell you about the quality of the files they produce.

Also note that if you have only one or two films it's not a good idea to purchase such a device for just one use.

42. THE ZIP DRIVE

The **Zip drive** was a type of floppy disk storage paired with a proportional drive by the company Iomega in 1994.

Initial capacity was of a 100 MB later 250 MB and the last models had a capacity of finally 750 MB.

Since late models had a USB interface the Zip drive unit can easily be connected even to a Windows 10 or Windows 11 PC without driver requirement.

It is also possible to be connected through IDE, SCSI and Firewire interfaces although in modern PC's you need a special PCI-E add-on card for these.

Picture 101. The Zip Drive

Photo by Wikipedia Commons

https://commons.wikimedia.org/wiki/File:ZIP_Drive_100,_2.jpg

More about it on the Wikipedia article:

https://en.wikipedia.org/wiki/Zip_drive

The Video Backup system or VHS Backer was nothing more than a device which allowed you to backup computer data to a VHS tape. No technological breakthrough here since back from the 50's computer data were stored on magnetic media.

Most of the 80's and early 90's home computers also (like Spectrum, Commodore, Amstrad, Atari etc.) were using audio cassette tapes for games and programs.

You have to do at least two backups of your data since a fault in the Video tape could result in an unspecified amount of data loss.

Last known mention of that system was two versions, one portable connected to the parallel port and one internal connected to a classic PCI Slot by a company called Danmere, now defunct. They claimed you could store up to 4GB in one videotape.

Back to those days 4GB of HDD storage was way too expensive but a VHS tape easily affordable. With the data loss risk of course as mentioned.

Try their site on www.webarchive.org

https://web.archive.org/web/20000511064400fw_/http://www.danmere.com/backerindex.htm

You could connect it also to other computer platforms like an Amiga computer as well with custom drivers.

Last supported Windows version was the Windows 98. Not possible to know if you could connect it to a modern PC since the device itself is extremely rare to find, supposing of course that the tape itself is undamaged.

Here is an advertisement from a PC Magazine back in 1999

Danmere Backer 32

Even if you've upgraded to DVD, you may want to reconsider tossing your old VCR. Danmere blows the doors off traditional backup solutions with Backup 32, a cheap and convenient way of backing up a maximum of 4GB of data onto a standard VHS cassette. We're not making this up. Offered in external and internal versions, Backup 32 allows you to store data on VHS, SVHS, Video8, camcorder, and Betamax tapes. A typical four-hour VHS tape can hold up to 2GB of data in normal mode and 4GB in long-play mode. Throughput is up to 9MB/min, so backing up a gigabyte of data would take at least an hour. The external version of Backer 32 connects via parallel port and includes a printer pass-through. Both the external and internal versions connect to the VCR or camcorder using standard composite video cables. Danmere; www.danmere.com; $89 external, $69 internal;

Back up 4GB on your old VCR!

Picture 102. VHS Backer Advertisement

There is also a Youtube Video with review of the backer on the LGR Oddware

https://www.youtube.com/watch?v=TUS0Zv2APjU

Picture 103. VHS Backer Review by LGR Oddware – Screenshot from Youtube Video

44. TAPE BACKUP OR TAPE STREAMER

The Tape Backup was another type of magnetic media backup that dates back to 1951.

Some models only were targeted for home or small office use, like the DEC Tx87 of 1993 with capacity of 20GB with SCSI Interface. For such old drives even if the tapes are intact there are no sufficient information if you can connect and access the data on a modern PC, even with a SCSI Adapter.

Also, almost any other drive requires a specific type of tape which makes things even more difficult.

If you think that the times of magnetic media are long over by now, well it's not. That Tape Backup technology is still in development with latest models, the 2018 IBM TS1160 with capacity of 20TB and that Linear Tape-Open of 2021, with current version LTO-9 capacity, 18 TB.

LTO will be developed further with the LTO-14 version to be capable of having 1,440 TB capacity.

That is an unimaginable size considering that currently in 2023 largest HDD capacity is at 22TB the SSD at 100TB (although consumer SSD largest size is 8TB) and a four-layer Blu-ray disk is 128GB.

95

All these new models are using for connection the Thunderbold for Mac and the SAS PCIe Raid Controller for Windows. They are targeted for Industrial / Professional use only, with target price of the drive, beginning at 2500$.

For the Thunderbolt connection interface, check here:

https://en.wikipedia.org/wiki/Thunderbolt_(interface)

and for the SAS (Serial Attached SCSI) interface here:

https://en.wikipedia.org/wiki/Serial_Attached_SCSI

Picture 104. DDS tape drive. Above, from left to right: DDS-4 tape (20 GB), 112m Data8 tape (2.5 GB), QIC DC-6250 tape (250 MB), and a 3.5" floppy disk (1.44 MB).

Photo by Wikipedia commons

https://en.wikipedia.org/wiki/Tape_drive#/media/File:Dds_tape_drive_01.jpg

More about it on the Wikipedia article:

https://en.wikipedia.org/wiki/Tape_drive

EPILOGUE

As we have observed, digitization, and most importantly the classification and documentation of material, is a time consuming and extremely demanding process.

Moving the material into modern and readable forms, documenting it and delivering it to future generations is the ultimate goal, and we have seen that it is fully and efficiently achieved.

The challenges are many and continuous, and professional digitization, which is still in its early stages of standardization, will expand to many more areas and applications in the future.

It is up to us to preserve the digital heritage of our nation, but also our own, hidden in boxes and drawers.

The knowledge is there, the infrastructure is also, and all that is needed is the will and the organization.

On account of these considerations, I believe that with this book I have contributed to this.